Life in the UK Test
Practice Questions

**Questions and answers for the
British citizenship test**

....

Published by Red Squirrel Publishing

Red Squirrel Publishing
Suite 235, 77 Beak Street,
London W1F 9DB, United Kingdom

www.redsquirrelbooks.com

First edition published in 2006
Fourth edition – Third impression

ISBN: 978-1-907389-19-1

Edited by Henry Dillon and George Sandison

Designed and artworked by
Cox Design Limited, Witney, Oxon

Printed by Cambrian in the UK

CONTENTS

INTRODUCTION

The Life in the UK Test is an essential part of the process for anyone planning on becoming a British citizen or applying for Indefinite Leave to Remain. Passing the test is compulsory under the 'Knowledge of life and language in the UK' requirement of your application.

Before October 2013, if you have passed the Life in the UK Test you meet the knowledge of life and language requirement. However, if you make your application on or after 28 October 2013, you will be required to both pass the Life in the UK Test and also have a speaking and listening qualification in English at B1 Common European Framework of Reference for Languages (CEFR) or higher, or its equivalent. Exceptions are made for applicants from majority English-speaking countries.

Over 150,000 people take the Life in the UK Test every year but not all of them pass. With each attempt costing £50, this can be an expensive and timely mistake. However, with the right preparation, you can be one of those who passes first time.

About this book

This book is designed to test your knowledge and understanding of the official study materials. This introduction offers advice on how to prepare for the test and guidance on the kinds of question you will face in your test.

There are 20 complete practice tests, each containing 24 questions in the same format as the actual test. The questions are all based on the testable sections of the official study materials, and these are the following chapters:

- The values and principles of the UK

- What is the UK?

- A long and illustrious history

- A modern, thriving society

- The UK government, the law and your role.

You should read all of this introduction before you take any practice tests to help you prepare and understand all of the features of this book.

Take some time to read through the following sections carefully. They tell you about all the features of this book and will enable you to get as much out of it as possible.

How to prepare for the test

1. Study the materials

The first and most important step of your preparations is to study the complete official study materials. These are found in the Home Office handbook, *Life in the United Kingdom: A Guide for New Residents* and are reproduced in our titles, *Life in the UK Test: Study Guide* and *Handbook*. You can find more information about these books at **www.lifeintheuk.net/studyguide**

It is essential that you read and understand the testable chapters before taking your test. Taking practice tests alone will not prepare you for the real test.

2. Take practice tests

Once you've finished thoroughly reviewing the study materials, you should check if you are ready to take the test by completing several practice tests from this book.

When you sit your official test, you will be given 45 minutes to complete the test. So when you take a practice test, you should allow yourself the same time. The pass mark in the official test is at least 75% – or only six incorrect answers. Again, this is what you should aim to score when you take a practice test.

If you can consistently score at least 75% and finish a test within 45 minutes, then you are ready to take your official test.

If you do not pass the practice tests satisfactorily and do not feel confident enough to sit your official test, then you should continue your study of the testable materials. If you do not have sufficient time left before your official test to do more study, then you may be able to reschedule your test appointment. You can reschedule your test without charge up to seven days before the date. If you cancel your booking with less than seven days' notice, your booking fee will not be refunded.

3. Online tests

Once you've finished testing yourself using the questions in this book, you can go online and access further tests with our free subscription offer.

Visit **www.lifeintheuk.net/test** and register an account to redeem this offer.

WARNING: DO NOT MEMORISE QUESTIONS

The practice questions contained in this book are intended to help you assess your understanding of the study materials and check if you are ready to take the official test.

Do not prepare for the test by memorising the questions in this book.

All the questions are in the same format as the official test questions. But they are not identical to the questions in the official test. The Home Office regularly revises the wording of questions used in the Life in the UK Test.

It is very important that you fully read and understand the study materials before taking your test.

SEND US YOUR FEEDBACK

Our books have helped thousands of people pass the Life in the UK Test. So we're always delighted when we hear from our readers. You can send us your comments by visiting **www.lifeintheuk.net/feedback**

CHECKLIST

There are a lot of things that you need to remember to do for the Life in the UK Test. Avoid problems and get organised by completing this checklist.

☐ Test appointment booked

Book your test through the UKBA website **www.lituktestbooking.co.uk** or by calling the Life in the UK Test Helpline on **0800 015 4245**

Test Date   Time

Test Centre Address

Phone

☐ Finished reading study materials

☐ Completed all practice tests in this book

☐ Completed free online practice tests at **www.lifeintheuk.net**

☐ Checked latest tips and advice at **www.lifeintheuk.net**

☐ Checked your registered details exactly match your photo ID

☐ Checked your proof of address is valid

☐ Confirmed test centre location and travel route

QUESTIONS TO EXPECT

All questions in the Life in the UK Test are multiple-choice. There are four different formats in which a question may be asked:

1. One correct answer – Choose the correct answer to the question from four options

EXAMPLE

What important event in the development of women's rights happened in 1928?

- **A** Women were first given the right to vote.
- **B** Women were given the right to vote at the same age as men.
- **C** The first divorce laws were introduced.
- **D** Women were allowed to keep their own earnings and property.

2. Two correct answers – Choose two correct answers to the question from four options

EXAMPLE

Which TWO of the following are famous Paralympians?

- **A** Baroness Tanni Grey-Thompson
- **B** Dame Kelly Holmes
- **C** Jayne Torvill
- **D** Ellie Simmonds

3. True or False – Decide whether a statement is true or false

EXAMPLE

Is the statement below TRUE or FALSE?
A newspaper's owner may try to influence government policy by running a campaign

- **A** True
- **B** False

4. **Select correct statement – Choose the correct statement from two options**

EXAMPLE

Which of these statements is correct?

   A Florence Nightingale is often regarded as the founder of modern nursing.

   B Florence Nightingale pioneered the use of syringes in hospitals.

Working through the answers

When you start your test, make sure you read each question carefully. Make sure you understand it.

If you are confident that you know the correct answer, make your selection and move on to the next question.

It is vital that you select an answer for every question even if you are not confident that it is correct. There is a chance that even a guess will be correct! If you do this, make sure that you note the question number on your blank paper. It is possible that a question later in the test will help you to answer a question that you have found difficult.

Traps to watch out for

Some questions may be worded so that an option may be a TRUE statement but not be the CORRECT answer to the question being asked.

Be careful if questions and answers use words that are absolute. These words mean that the question or answer applies in all cases (e.g. *always, every*) or not at all (e.g. *never*).

EXAMPLE

Which of the following statements is correct?

   A There are a few members of Parliament who do not represent any of the main political parties.

   B All members of Parliament have to belong to a political party.

The second statement is absolute. There are no exceptions. This means the correct answer is A because, whether or not there are currently independent members of Parliament (MPs) in Parliament, there *can* be independent MPs in Parliament.

You also need to be careful of words that *moderate* a question or answer. When words such as *often, rarely, sometimes* and *usually* are used, this means that the question or answer is referring to something that is not true in all cases.

EXAMPLE

Who usually chooses who will be the Archbishop of Canterbury?

A The monarch

B The Prime Minister and a committee appointed by the Church

C A committee appointed by the Church

D The Prime Minister

In the above example, all of the options could be correct. The monarch has the right to choose, but does not in practice. Whilst both a committee appointed by the Church and the Prime Minister are both usually involved in the decision. This means that C and D are accurate, but not correct because they don't provide a full answer. B is the only answer that fully answers the question.

Also watch for negative words in questions or answers – such as *not, never* and *neither*. These words can be easily overlooked and completely change the meaning of the question being asked.

EXAMPLE

Which of these socially progressive measures was not introduced during the early years of the 20th century?

A Free school meals

B Old-age pensions

C Financial help for the unemployed

D Equal pay for women

In the example above, notice that the question is asking for the statement that is not correct. Free school meals, old-age pensions and financial help for the unemployed were all introduced at the start of the 20th century. There are no laws enforcing equal pay conditions for women in the UK, however. Therefore, although option D is a false statement, it is the correct answer for this question.

For some questions, one of the answers may read: 'All of the above'. In these cases, read the other answers carefully to see if it is possible that they are all correct. Even if two of the three answers seem correct, all three alternative answers must be correct for you to choose the 'all of the above' option.

For some questions, one of the answers may read: 'None of the above'. In these cases, read the other answers carefully to see if it is possible that they are all incorrect. Even if two of the three answers seem incorrect, all three alternative answers must be wrong for you to choose the 'none of the above' option.

PRACTICE TEST 1

1   Who did Henry VIII marry after the execution of Anne Boleyn?

- **A**   Catherine Howard
- **B**   Catherine Parr
- **C**   Anne of Cleves
- **D**   Jane Seymour

2   How old was Edward VI when he died?

- **A**   15
- **B**   18
- **C**   56
- **D**   35

3   Scotland changed in which TWO ways after the Battle of Culloden?

- **A**   Chieftains became landlords if they had the favour of the English king
- **B**   Chieftains took control of the land away from the English king
- **C**   Clansmen became tenants who had to pay for the land they used
- **D**   The clans were entirely destroyed

4   The Battle of the Boyne is celebrated with a bank holiday in which country?

- **A**   England
- **B**   Wales
- **C**   Northern Ireland
- **D**   Scotland

5 **Which TWO of the following are famous British landmarks?**

    A The London Eye

    B Albert Square

    C The Eden Project

    D The Smithsonian

6 **Which country of the UK is not represented on the Union Flag?**

    A Scotland

    B Wales

    C Northern Ireland

    D England

7 **Which of these people was a great British playwright?**

    A Sir Francis Drake

    B Geoffrey Chaucer

    C William Caxton

    D William Shakespeare

8 **Which of these statements is correct?**

    A Refuges and shelters offer a safe place to stay for victims of domestic violence.

    B The Citizens Advice Bureau offers a safe place to stay for victims of domestic violence.

9 **When were the first professional football clubs formed?**

    A 17th century

    B 18th century

    C 19th century

    D 20th century

10 Which work of music did Benjamin Britten not write?

- **A** Peter Grimes
- **B** The Planets
- **C** Billy Budd
- **D** A Young Person's Guide to the Orchestra

11 Which of the following countries did not help to set up the EEC?

- **A** Ireland
- **B** Luxemburg
- **C** Belgium
- **D** Germany

12 Which of the following is a good way of helping your community?

- **A** Travelling
- **B** Complaining
- **C** Volunteering
- **D** Spending lots of time online

13 How are local authorities funded?

- **A** By funding from central government only
- **B** By taxation only
- **C** By central government funding and by taxation
- **D** Local authorities are unfunded

14 Is the statement below TRUE or FALSE?
Discrimination in the workplace is an example of criminal law.

- **A** True
- **B** False

15 Which of these statements is correct?

- **A** Everyone pays National Insurance Contributions.
- **B** Most working people pay National Insurance Contributions.

16 Who did William the Conqueror defeat at the Battle of Hastings in 1066?

- **A** King Cnut
- **B** Boudicca
- **C** Kenneth MacAlpin
- **D** King Harold

17 Which British novelist created the fictional detective, Sherlock Holmes?

- **A** Sir Arthur Conan Doyle
- **B** Evelyn Waugh
- **C** Robert Louis Stevenson
- **D** Graham Greene

18 What sport is played in the UEFA Champions League?

- **A** Tennis
- **B** Rugby
- **C** Football
- **D** Cricket

19 Who chairs debates in the House of Commons?

- **A** The leader of the opposition
- **B** The Prime Minister
- **C** The Speaker
- **D** The Foreign Secretary

20 **Which of these is an accurate estimate of the number of casualties suffered by Britain in the First World War?**

- **A** 2 million
- **B** 10 million
- **C** 8 million
- **D** 500,000

21 **William Shakespeare wrote a number of sonnets. What are sonnets?**

- **A** Poems of 14 lines
- **B** Mystery plays
- **C** Rhyming poems
- **D** Stories for children

22 **Is the statement below TRUE or FALSE?**
Population growth in the UK has been faster in recent years, thanks in part to migration and longer life expectancy.

- **A** True
- **B** False

23 **How old do you have to be to buy alcohol in the UK?**

- **A** 16
- **B** 18
- **C** 20
- **D** 21

24 **Who is the patron saint of Scotland?**

- **A** St David
- **B** St George
- **C** St Patrick
- **D** St Andrew

ANSWERS: PRACTICE TEST 1

			Handbook reference	Study Guide reference
1	D	Jane Seymour	41	47
2	A	15	42	48
3	A	Chieftains became landlords if they had the favour of the English king	52	58
	C	Clansmen became tenants who had to pay for the land they used		
4	C	Northern Ireland	91	97
5	A	The London Eye	113–21	119–27
	C	The Eden Project		
6	B	Wales	58	64
7	D	William Shakespeare	44	50
8	A	Refuges and shelters offer a safe place to stay for victims of domestic violence.	154	160
9	C	19th century	94–5	100–1
10	B	The Planets	98	104
11	A	Ireland	142	148
12	C	Volunteering	159	165
13	C	By central government funding and by taxation	133	139
14	B	False	144–5	150–1
15	B	Most working people pay National Insurance Contributions.	156	162
16	D	King Harold	33	39
17	A	Sir Arthur Conan Doyle	104	110
18	C	Football	94–5	100–1
19	C	The Speaker	129–30	135–6
20	A	2 million	65	71
21	A	Poems of 14 lines	104–6	110–2
22	A	True	82–3	88–9
23	B	18	144–5	150–1
24	D	St Andrew	85–6	91–2

PRACTICE TEST 2

1   Is the statement below TRUE or FALSE?
    Military training for young people is provided
    by The National Citizen Service.

   A True

   B False

2   MPs have a duty to serve and represent
    which of the following groups?

   A Their fellow MPs

   B Everyone in their constituency

   C Everyone in their constituency who voted for them

   D The House of Lords

3   Which of the following statements is correct?

   A During the Industrial Revolution, canals were built to link
         the mines in the mountains with factories in the cities.

   B During the Industrial Revolution, canals were built
         to link the factories to cities and ports.

4   An attempt by which group to put James II's son on the
    throne instead of George I was quickly defeated?

   A French Huguenots

   B Scottish Jacobites

   C Irish Catholics

   D English Puritans

5   Is the statement below TRUE or FALSE?
    The Bill of Rights confirmed the rights of Parliament
    and the limits of the king's power.

   A True

   B False

6   Charles I was unwilling to reach an agreement with Parliament. Following his defeat in the Civil War, what happened to him?

    A He was exiled

    B He was executed

    C He was exonerated

    D He was excommunicated

7   Is the statement below TRUE or FALSE?
Following the Emancipation Act of 1833, the Royal Navy stopped slave ships from other countries and freed the slaves

    A True

    B False

8   Is the statement below TRUE or FALSE?
Lands taken from Catholics in 17th-century Ireland and given to Protestant settlers were known as 'plantations'.

    A True

    B False

9   Which of the following provide legal advice, normally for a fee?

    A Judges

    B Magistrates

    C Solicitors

    D The police

10   Is the statement below TRUE or FALSE?
Some people rent land away from home called an allotment, where they can grow fruit and vegetables.

    A True

    B False

11 Which of these statements is true?

- **A** Most people live in towns and cities but much of Britain is still countryside.

- **B** Most people live in the countryside but much of Britain is covered by towns and cities.

12 During the reign of Henry VIII, which country of the union became formally united with England?

- **A** Ireland

- **B** Wales

- **C** Scotland

- **D** Northern Ireland

13 The judiciary is responsible for which TWO of the following?

- **A** Interpreting the law

- **B** Making the law

- **C** Arresting people

- **D** Making sure that trials are fair

14 Is the statement below TRUE or FALSE?
Norman French influenced the development of the English language as we know it today.

- **A** True

- **B** False

15 Which of the following statements is not correct?

- **A** The attack on Normandy by Allied forces is often called D-Day.

- **B** D-Day was an Allied operation that attacked German forces in France by advancing through Spain.

16 **Which annual flower show in London exhibits garden designs from around the world?**

   A South Bank

   B Covent Garden

   C Chelsea

   D Kensington

17 **Where did the people of the Bronze Age bury their dead?**

   A Round burrows

   B Round barrows

   C Burial mounds

   D Earth barrows

18 **In a Crown Court, who decides what the penalty will be, in the case of a 'guilty' verdict?**

   A A solicitor

   B The judge

   C The jury

   D A police officer

19 **What event in 1851 took place at the Crystal Palace in Hyde Park and showed goods and exhibits from Britain and across the world.**

   A The Great Exhibition

   B The Great Show

   C The Great Event

   D The Great Occasion

20 **Sake Dean Mahomet opened which establishment in George Street, London in 1810?**

A Hindoostane Coffee House

B Pakistan Curry House

C Mahomet Coffee House

D Mahomet Shampoo Parlour

21 **Which of these is not a Christmas tradition in the UK?**

A Giving gifts

B Having a barbecue

C Sending cards

D Decorating houses and trees

22 **Catherine Parr married Henry VIII late in his life. Who died first?**

A She died first and he never remarried

B He died first and she was a widow for the rest of her life

C She died in childbirth and Henry remarried

D He died first and she went on to remarry

23 **Which of the following statements is correct?**

A Elizabeth I came to the throne when, following a short reign, her half-sister Mary died.

B Elizabeth I came to the throne when, following a long reign, her cousin Mary died.

24 **Who wrote musicals such as Cats, The Phantom of the Opera and Evita?**

A Sir Edward Elgar

B Gilbert and Sullivan

C Andrew Lloyd Webber

D Julian Lloyd Webber

ANSWERS: PRACTICE TEST 2

			Handbook reference	Study Guide reference
1	B	False	162–4	167–71
2	B	Everyone in their constituency	130	136
3	B	During the Industrial Revolution, canals were built to link the factories to cities and ports.	53–5	59–61
4	B	Scottish Jacobites	52	58
5	A	True	51	57
6	B	He was executed	46–8	52–4
7	A	True	55–6	61–2
8	A	True	45	51
9	C	Solicitors	152–3	158–9
10	A	True	106–7	112–3
11	A	Most people live in towns and cities but much of Britain is still countryside.	80	86
12	B	Wales	40–2	46–8
13	A	Interpreting the law	147–8	153–4
	D	Making sure that trials are fair		
14	A	True	33–4	39–40
15	B	D-Day was an Allied operation that attacked German forces in France by advancing through Spain.	66–9	72–5
16	C	Chelsea	102–3	108–9
17	B	Round barrows	30–1	36–7
18	B	The judge	148	154
19	A	The Great Exhibition	59–60	65–66
20	A	Hindoostane Coffee House	55	61
21	B	Having a barbecue	87	93
22	D	He died first and she went on to remarry	41	47
23	A	Elizabeth I came to the throne when, following a short reign, her half-sister Mary died.	40–2	46–8
24	C	Andrew Lloyd Webber	99–100	105–6

PRACTICE TEST 3

1 Which of the following statements is correct?

A The Wimbledon Championships are associated with athletics.

B The Wimbledon Championships are associated with tennis.

2 The last successful foreign invasion of England was by which of the following?

A The Romans led by Julius Caesar

B The Romans led by Emperor Claudius

C The Vikings

D The Normans led by William

3 Is the statement below TRUE or FALSE?
Mary Peters was an author who was later made a Dame in recognition of her work promoting literacy.

A True

B False

4 Where does the UK Parliament sit?

A Westminster

B Downing Street

C Stormont

D The House of Lords

5 Which of the following statements is correct?

A The 'Divine Right of Kings' was the view held by many English monarchs that they could seize lands belonging to the nobility as they wished.

B The 'Divine Right of Kings' was the view held by many English monarchs that they were directly appointed by God to rule.

6   George Frederick Handel, the German-born composer who became a British citizen, wrote which of the following?

○ **A**   Balthazar's Feast

○ **B**   Peter Grimes

○ **C**   The Planets

○ **D**   Music for the Royal Fireworks

7   The Wars of the Roses was fought by the supporters of which TWO families in order to decide who should be King of England?

○ **A**   The House of Lancaster

○ **B**   The House of Windsor

○ **C**   The House of York

○ **D**   The House of Tudor

8   Which famous leader said the following:
'We shall fight on the beaches, we shall fight on the landing grounds, we shall fight in the fields and in the streets, we shall fight in the hills; we shall never surrender'?

○ **A**   Admiral Nelson

○ **B**   Winston Churchill

○ **C**   Clement Attlee

○ **D**   Oliver Cromwell

9   Are police obliged to obey the law?

○ **A**   Yes, except when investigating a difficult case

○ **B**   Yes, always

10   Which of the following is not an aim of the United Nations?

○ **A**   To promote peace

○ **B**   To promote international security

○ **C**   To prevent war

○ **D**   To promote free trade

11 How often is a General Election held?

- **A** Every year
- **B** At least every two years
- **C** At least every four years
- **D** At least every five years

12 After his campaign in Ireland and his defeat of Charles II, Oliver Cromwell was given what title?

- **A** King
- **B** Lord Lieutenant
- **C** Lord Protector
- **D** Chieftain

13 Which of the following statements is correct?

- **A** The Black Death destroyed cereal crops, leading to a famine that killed many peasants.
- **B** After the Black Death, there were labour shortages and peasants began to demand higher wages.

14 What is the capital city of Northern Ireland?

- **A** Belfast
- **B** Dublin
- **C** The Pale
- **D** Edinburgh

15 What is New Year's Eve called in Scotland?

- **A** Hopmanay
- **B** Hogmanay
- **C** Hagmanay
- **D** Hugmanay

16 Who or what were the 'clans'?

   A English lords

   B Welsh landowners

   C Prominent families in Scotland and Ireland

   D Prominent families in England and Wales

17 Who was James II's eldest daughter, Mary, married to?

   A William of Orange

   B The Duke of York

   C The French Dauphin

   D She never married

18 Britain was brought into conflict with which country during the 19th century, because they were expanding and trading in similar areas?

   A Germany

   B The Netherlands

   C Spain

   D France

19 Which 1935 film was directed by Alfred Hitchcock?

   A The 21 Steps

   B The 39 Steps

   C The 100 Steps

   D The 1,001 Steps

20 Is the statement below TRUE or FALSE?
Members of the House of Lords are elected by a constituency.

   A True

   B False

21 Who wrote the novel Lucky Jim?

   A James Joyce

   B Sir Kingsley Amis

   C James Callaghan

   D Jimmy Tarbuck

22 Which of these statements is correct?

   A The United Kingdom consists of England, Ireland, Scotland and Wales.

   B The United Kingdom consists of England, Scotland, Wales and Northern Ireland.

23 Which TWO of the following are amongst the shared goals of the Commonwealth?

   A Development

   B Dependency

   C Democracy

   D Discrimination

24 Which of the following is one of the Queen's important ceremonial roles?

   A To chair debates in Parliament

   B To write laws

   C To receive foreign ambassadors and high commissioners

   D To negotiate trade agreements with other countries

ANSWERS: PRACTICE TEST 3

			Handbook reference	Study Guide reference
1	B	The Wimbledon Championships are associated with tennis.	96	102
2	D	The Normans led by William	33–44	39–40
3	B	False	75	81
4	A	Westminster	26	32
5	B	The 'Divine Right of Kings' was the view held by many English monarchs that they were directly appointed by God to rule.	45–6	51–2
6	D	Music for the Royal Fireworks	97–9	103–5
7	A	The House of Lancaster	39	45
	C	The House of York		
8	B	Winston Churchill	68	74
9	B	Yes, always	145–6	151–2
10	D	To promote free trade	143	149
11	D	At least every five years	130	136
12	C	Lord Protector	46–8	52–4
13	B	After the Black Death, there were labour shortages and peasants began to demand higher wages.	35–6	41–2
14	A	Belfast	81	87
15	B	Hogmanay	53	59
16	C	Prominent families in Scotland and Ireland	35	41
17	A	William of Orange	49–50	55–6
18	D	France	53–5	59–61
19	B	The 39 Steps	109	115
20	B	False	129	135
21	B	Sir Kingsley Amis	104	110
22	B	The United Kingdom consists of England, Scotland, Wales and Northern Ireland.	26	32
23	A	Development	141	147
	C	Democracy		
24	C	To receive foreign ambassadors and high commissioners	125–7	131–3

PRACTICE TEST 4

1   **Is the statement below TRUE or FALSE?**
Under the system of feudalism, the kings gave land to lords, and the landowners had to send men to serve in the army in return.

A True

B False

2   **Is a verdict of 'not proven' possible?**

A Yes, but only in a Magistrates' Court

B Yes, but only in Scotland

3   **Is the statement below TRUE or FALSE?**
Jane Austen and Charles Dickens were both famous sculptors.

A True

B False

4   **Is the statement below TRUE or FALSE?**
The Council of Europe has the power to make laws, which are binding in member states.

A True

B False

5   **Is the statement below TRUE or FALSE?**
Adult citizens of other EU states may vote in General Elections.

A True

B False

6 **After the Act of Union, Scotland was no longer an independent country. In what TWO ways was it still separate from the rest of Great Britain?**

A It kept its own army

B It kept its own educational system

C It kept its Presbyterian Church

D Hadrian's Wall was rebuilt to secure the border

7 **Which of the following statements is correct?**

A A dog's owner is responsible for keeping the animal under control and cleaning up after it in public places.

B A dog's owner is responsible for keeping it under control, but doesn't have to clean up after it in public places.

8 **Is the statement below TRUE or FALSE?**
Richard Arkwright developed horse-driven spinning mills that used only one machine, increasing efficiency and production.

A True

B False

9 **Which of these books did Graham Greene not write?**

A The Honorary Consul

B Brighton Rock

C Moby Dick

D The Heart of the Matter

10 **Who were Elizabeth I's parents?**

A Henry VII and Elizabeth of York

B Henry VIII and Catherine of Aragon

C Henry VIII and Jane Seymour

D Henry VIII and Anne Boleyn

11 **In 1948 Aneurin (Nye) Bevan led the establishment of the National Health Service (NHS). What was his role at the time?**

A Minister for Health

B Deputy Prime Minister

C Home Secretary

D Minister for Social Security

12 **What was the main source of employment in the UK before the Industrial Revolution?**

A Agriculture

B The wool trade

C Financial services

D Canal building

13 **Which of the following statements is correct?**

A The jet engine and radar were developed in Britain in the 1950s.

B The jet engine and radar were developed in Britain in the 1930s.

14 **Is the statement below TRUE or FALSE?**
By around AD 600, Anglo-Saxon kingdoms were established in Britain.

A True

B False

15 **In 1649, England was declared a republic. What was it called?**

A The Commonwealth

B The People's Republic

C Cromwell's Republic

D Great Britain

16 Which TWO of the following were members of the Royal Society?

A Sir Christopher Wren

B Samuel Pepys

C Sir Edmond Halley

D Sir Isaac Newton

17 Is it acceptable in the UK to treat people worse because of their sexual orientation?

A Yes, if their sexual orientation is forbidden by religion

B No, it is never acceptable to treat people worse for their sexual orientation

18 Queen Elizabeth II is the head of state for which TWO of the following?

A The United Kingdom

B The European Union

C Iceland

D Many Commonwealth countries

19 Is the statement below TRUE or FALSE?
Sir Robert Walpole was Prime Minister from 1700–1730.

A True

B False

20 A snack made from flour, dried fruits and spices and served either hot or cold is which of the following?

A A Scottish bun

B An English muffin

C An Irish pie

D A Welsh cake

21 **What is the name of the famous horse race held near Liverpool?**

- **A** Grand Chase
- **B** Grand Derby
- **C** Steeplechase
- **D** Grand National

22 **NATO is a group of North American and European countries that have agreed to do which TWO of the following?**

- **A** Promote peace between member countries
- **B** Promote traditional culture
- **C** Protect each other when under attack
- **D** Allow the free movement of people across borders

23 **Is the statement below TRUE or FALSE?**
Commercial expansion and prosperity of the 18th century were sustained in part by the booming slave trade.

- **A** True
- **B** False

24 **Is the statement below TRUE or FALSE?**
You have to be 16 or over to buy a drink in a public house (pub) or nightclub.

- **A** True
- **B** False

ANSWERS: PRACTICE TEST 4

			Handbook reference	Study Guide reference
1	A	True	35–6	41–2
2	B	Yes, but only in Scotland	148	154
3	B	False	104	110
4	B	False	143	149
5	B	False	138	144
6	B	It kept its own educational system	52	58
	C	It kept its Presbyterian Church		
7	A	A dog's owner is responsible for keeping the animal under control and cleaning up after it in public places.	112	118
8	A	True	54	60
9	C	Moby Dick	104	110
10	D	Henry VIII and Anne Boleyn	40–2	46–8
11	A	Minister for Health	70–1	76–7
12	A	Agriculture	53–5	59–61
13	B	The jet engine and radar were developed in Britain in the 1930s.	74–5	80–1
14	A	True	31–3	37–9
15	A	The Commonwealth	46–8	52–4
16	C	Sir Edmond Halley	48	54
	D	Sir Isaac Newton		
17	B	No, it is never acceptable to treat people worse for their sexual orientation	158	164
18	A	The United Kingdom	125–7	131–3
	D	Many Commonwealth countries		
19	B	False	52	58
20	D	A Welsh cake	108	114
21	D	Grand National	95	101
22	A	Promote peace between member countries	143	149
	C	Protect each other when under attack		
23	A	True	55–6	61–2
24	B	False	111	117

PRACTICE TEST 5

1 **Is the statement below TRUE or FALSE?**
   *The police do not need to protect and help
   people who are not UK citizens.*

   A True

   B False

2 **Is the statement below TRUE or FALSE?**
   The Channel Islands and the Isle of Man are part of the UK.

   A True

   B False

3 **Is the statement below TRUE or FALSE?**
   *The Puritans agreed with the religious reforms of the
   Church of England introduced by Charles I.*

   A True

   B False

4 **Which Catherine was executed after being
   accused of taking lovers by Henry VIII?**

   A Parr

   B Boleyn

   C Of Aragon

   D Howard

5 **Someone wishing to stand as a candidate for election
   as an MP would need to be how old?**

   A 16

   B 18

   C 21

   D There is no minimum age limit

6   Sir Anthony Van Dyck was famous as which of the following?

  A Actor

  B Painter

  C Sculptor

  D Composer

7   Which of the following takes place on 14 February every year?

  A St Christopher's Day

  B St George's Day

  C St Valentine's Day

  D All Saints Day

8   Which of the following statements is correct?

  A Chequers is the Prime Minister's country house.

  B Chequers is the Prime Minister's house in London.

9   Where did Florence Nightingale establish the Nightingale School for Nurses in 1860?

  A St Thomas' Hospital, London

  B Addenbrooke's Hospital, Cambridge

  C St James's University Hospital, Leeds

  D Prince Philip Hospital, Llanelli

10   What are small Scottish farms also known as?

  A Crofts

  B Bothies

  C Hamlets

  D Homesteads

11 Ian McEwan, Hilary Mantel and Julian Barnes have all won which literary prize?

- **A** The Turner Prize
- **B** The Man Booker Prize
- **C** The Nobel Prize in Literature
- **D** The Mercury Prize

12 For much of the Stone Age, Britain was connected to the continent by what?

- **A** A bridge
- **B** A land bridge
- **C** A glacier
- **D** A tunnel

13 Which of the following statements is correct?

- **A** Pantomimes are usually based on fairy stories.
- **B** Pantomimes are usually based on famous events from history.

14 In what way was Elizabeth I skilled at managing Parliament?

- **A** She established a balance between Catholics and Protestants by not persecuting either group
- **B** She reduced the power of Parliament so her wishes had more significance

15 The National Assembly makes laws for Wales in 20 areas. It does not make laws in which of the following areas?

- **A** Housing
- **B** Economic policy
- **C** Education and training
- **D** Health and social services

16 **Diwali is a religious celebration for which TWO religious groups?**

   A Jews

   B Muslims

   C Sikhs

   D Hindus

17 **Is the statement below TRUE or FALSE?**
In the Middle Ages, England's system of 'common law' was established by referring to previous decisions and tradition.

   A True

   B False

18 **Who became Prime Minister in May 2010?**

   A David Cameron

   B Nick Clegg

   C Ed Miliband

   D Nigel Farage

19 **Which Hindu and Sikh festival is normally celebrated in October or November every year?**

   A Diwali

   B Vaisakhi

   C Eid ul Adha

   D Hannukah

20 **Is the statement below TRUE or FALSE?**
The small claims procedure is an informal way for people to settle minor disputes.

   A True

   B False

21 What event is commemorated on 5 November every year?

- **A** England's World Cup victory of 1966
- **B** The end of the First World War
- **C** A plot to blow up the Houses of Parliament
- **D** The Queen's birthday

22 What is Ridley Scott famous for?

- **A** Directing films
- **B** Theatre production
- **C** Conducting orchestras
- **D** Singing as an operatic tenor

23 Is the statement below TRUE or FALSE?
The UK is a parliamentary democracy.

- **A** True
- **B** False

24 Which of the following statements is correct?

- **A** Murder, assault and theft are crimes.
- **B** Murder, assault and theft are examples of civil disputes.

ANSWERS: PRACTICE TEST 5

			Handbook reference	Study Guide reference
1	B	False	145–6	151–2
2	B	False	26	32
3	B	False	46	52
4	D	Howard	41	47
5	B	18	132	138
6	B	Painter	100–1	106–7
7	C	St Valentine's Day	90	96
8	A	Chequers is the Prime Minister's country house.	131	137
9	A	St Thomas' Hospital, London	61	67
10	A	Crofts	52–3	58–9
11	B	The Man Booker Prize	103	109
12	B	A land bridge	30–1	36–7
13	A	Pantomimes are usually based on fairy stories.	99–100	105–6
14	A	She established a balance between Catholics and Protestants by not persecuting either group	45–6	51–2
15	B	Economic policy	133–7	139–43
16	C	Sikhs	88	94
	D	Hindus		
17	A	True	36–7	42–3
18	A	David Cameron	78	84
19	A	Diwali	88	94
20	A	True	151	157
21	C	A plot to blow up the Houses of Parliament	90	96
22	A	Directing films	108–9	114–5
23	A	True	128	134
24	A	Murder, assault and theft are crimes.	144–5	150–1

PRACTICE TEST 6

1 **Which period of British history saw the emergence of a national culture and identity?**

- **A** The Bronze Age
- **B** The Middle Ages
- **C** The Victorian period
- **D** The Tudor period

2 **What is the capital city of the UK?**

- **A** Birmingham
- **B** Liverpool
- **C** London
- **D** Sheffield

3 **Is the statement below TRUE or FALSE?**
Sir Steve Redgrave was the first man in the world to run a mile in under four minutes.

- **A** True
- **B** False

4 **How many people emigrated from the UK during Victoria's reign between 1853 and 1913?**

- **A** 100,000
- **B** 13 million
- **C** 500 million
- **D** 2 million

5 Which of the following statements is correct?

A The declaration of rights read at the coronation of William and Mary meant the monarch could no longer raise taxes or administer justice.

B The declaration of rights read at the coronation of William and Mary meant the monarch had absolute power to rule without the interference of Parliament.

6 Is the statement below TRUE or FALSE?
Sir Ian Botham captained the England rugby team.

A True

B False

7 Where did the Boer War take place?

A South Africa

B France

C England

D Turkey

8 Richard Arkwright used steam engines to do what?

A Pull carriages

B Power machinery

C Create electricity

D All of the above

9 Henry VIII took which title in relation to Ireland?

A Head

B King

C Lieutenant

D Commander

10 **Which of the following statements is correct?**

   A During the 16th century, the Scottish Parliament welcomed the authority of the Pope and Roman Catholic religious services became commonplace.

   B During the 16th century, the Scottish Parliament abolished the authority of the Pope and Roman Catholic religious services became illegal.

11 **Which of the following statements is correct?**

   A A Magistrates' Court deals with only the most serious criminal cases.

   B A Magistrates' Court deals with minor criminal offences.

12 **Eid al-Fitr celebrates the end of Ramadan. For how long before do Muslims fast?**

   A Five days

   B Two weeks

   C One month

   D Twenty-one days

13 **The National Eisteddfod is a major cultural festival that takes place in which country?**

   A England

   B Scotland

   C Wales

   D Northern Ireland

14 **Is the statement below TRUE or FALSE?**
The threat of Viking attack caused the peoples in the north to unite, and the term Scotland was used to describe that country.

   A True

   B False

15 **The British equivalent of the Oscars is hosted by BAFTA. For what do these initials stand?**

   A British Association of Film and Technical Appliances

   B British Academy of Film and Theatre Awards

   C British Academy of Film and Television Arts

   D British Awards for Film and Television Actors

16 **What information must always be entered on an electoral registration form?**

   A Only the names of adult men resident at the address

   B The names of everyone at the address

   C The names of all eligible voters who live at the address

   D Only the names of adult women resident at the address

17 **Who is the ceremonial head of the Commonwealth?**

   A The Prime Minister

   B The President of the USA

   C The Queen

   D The Prince of Wales

18 **The French Wars ended in 1815 when Napoleon was defeated by the Duke of Wellington at which battle?**

   A Battle of Waterloo

   B Battle of Trafalgar

   C Battle of Ostend

   D Battle of Naseby

19 **Which Anglo-Saxon poem tells of its hero's battles against monsters?**

   A Beowulf

   B The Fight at Finnsburh

   C Waldere

   D Deor

20 **Which of the following statements is correct?**

- **A** The UK experienced high levels of employment during the Great Depression of the 1930s.
- **B** During the Great Depression of the 1930s, parts of the UK experienced mass unemployment.

21 **To apply to become a permanent resident or citizen of the UK, you will need to be able to do which TWO of the following?**

- **A** Speak and read English
- **B** Speak and read Welsh
- **C** Have a good understanding of life in the UK
- **D** Speak more than one language

22 **Which of the following is a famous British film?**

- **A** Passport to Paddington
- **B** Passport to Portsmouth
- **C** Passport to Panama
- **D** Passport to Pimlico

23 **The right for every adult male and female to vote is usually known as what?**

- **A** Universal balloting
- **B** Universal democracy
- **C** Universal voting rights
- **D** Universal suffrage

24 **Every MP represents which of the following?**

- **A** A constituency
- **B** A county
- **C** A city
- **D** None of the above

ANSWERS: PRACTICE TEST 6

			Handbook reference	Study Guide reference
1	B	The Middle Ages	37–9	43–5
2	C	London	81	87
3	B	False	92–3	98–9
4	B	13 million	59	65
5	A	The declaration of rights read at the coronation of William and Mary meant the monarch could no longer raise taxes or administer justice.	51	57
6	B	False	92–3	98–9
7	A	South Africa	63	69
8	B	Power machinery	54	60
9	B	King	45	51
10	B	During the 16th century, the Scottish Parliament abolished the authority of the Pope and Roman Catholic religious services became illegal.	43	49
11	B	A Magistrates' Court deals with minor criminal offences.	148	154
12	C	One month	89	95
13	C	Wales	97–9	103–5
14	A	True	33	39
15	C	British Academy of Film and Television Arts	108–9	114–5
16	C	The names of all eligible voters who live at the address	138–9	144–5
17	C	The Queen	141	147
18	A	Battle of Waterloo	56–7	62–3
19	A	Beowulf	104–6	110–2
20	B	During the Great Depression of the 1930s, parts of the UK experienced mass unemployment.	66	72
21	A	Speak and read English	21–2	27–8
	C	Have a good understanding of life in the UK		
22	D	Passport to Pimlico	108–9	114–5
23	D	Universal suffrage	61–2	67–8
24	A	A constituency	128	134

PRACTICE TEST 7

1 Who were the Huguenots?

- A Roman Catholics
- B French Catholics
- C Dutch Protestants
- D French Protestants

2 Is this statement TRUE or FALSE?
There are now more women in high-level positions than ever before.

- A True
- B False

3 Who wrote the poem The Tyger?

- A William Wordsworth
- B William Blake
- C William Shakespeare
- D William Wallace

4 Which of the following statements is correct?

- A Robert Burns wrote only in Scots language.
- B Robert Burns wrote in Scots, English and a combination of both.

5 Since which year has the Prime Minister had the power to nominate life peers to the House of Lords?

- A 1925
- B 1958
- C 1999
- D 2012

6   Which of these statements is correct?

   A All the national saints' days are celebrated but only in Scotland and Northern Ireland are they official holidays.

   B All the national saints' days are celebrated but only in England and Wales are they official holidays.

7   Is it possible for parents or other community groups to open a free school?

   A Yes, in any part of the UK

   B Yes, but only in England

8   Which of the following will help you get along with your neighbours?

   A Only putting rubbish and recycling out on collection days

   B Having an untidy garden

   C Making lots of noise, especially late at night

   D Only introducing yourself to them after a year

9   Is the statement below TRUE or FALSE?
Cricket is the UK's most popular sport.

   A True

   B False

10   Since which year has the UK had a fully democratic voting system?

   A 1889

   B 1918

   C 1928

   D 1969

11 **The Welsh Assembly and the Scottish Parliament were formed in which year?**

- **A** 1997
- **B** 1999
- **C** 2003
- **D** 2008

12 **Is the statement below TRUE or FALSE?**
France was the first country to industrialise on a large scale.

- **A** True
- **B** False

13 **Which of these reasons best explains why town planning laws were tightened in the early 20th century?**

- **A** To protect the countryside
- **B** To stop skyscrapers being built
- **C** To allow for the building of new churches
- **D** To prevent the further development of slums

14 **Is the statement below TRUE or FALSE?**
Thanks to its position as the world's leading industrial nation during the 1800s, Britain was responsible for producing half of the world's coal, iron and cotton cloth.

- **A** True
- **B** False

15 **How often is Prime Minister's Questions held?**

- **A** Every day
- **B** Every day while Parliament is in session
- **C** Every week
- **D** Every week while Parliament is in session

16 Which of the following statements is correct?

A People in the UK are living longer than ever before.

B The average lifespan for UK residents is steadily decreasing.

17 The Royal Society was formed to promote what?

A Astronomy

B Natural knowledge

C Art

D Music

18 Who is the head of state?

A The President

B The Prime Minister

C Prince Philip

D The Queen

19 Which TWO events happened to the church in England following the restoration of Charles II?

A The Church of England was restored as the official Church

B The Puritans and Roman Catholics were kept out of power

C The Puritans grew in strength and number

D The Church of England was suppressed

20 What is it traditional to do on 1 April in the UK?

A Play musical instruments in the street

B Play jokes on each other

C Hunt for eggs

D Make pancakes

21 **Is the statement below TRUE or FALSE?**
You must always tell a canvasser how you intend to vote.

   A True

   B False

22 **Which of the following statements is correct?**

   A Margaret Thatcher was the UK's first female Prime Minister.

   B Margaret Thatcher was the UK's second female Prime Minister.

23 **Which of the following statements is correct?**

   A Thomas Chippendale was an 18th-century designer of furniture.

   B Sir Terence Conran was an 18th-century designer of furniture.

24 **John Petts was a Welshman famous in which of these TWO areas of art?**

   A Stained glass

   B Water colours

   C Engraving

   D Paintings of horses

ANSWERS: PRACTICE TEST 7

			Handbook reference	Study Guide reference
1	D	French Protestants	52	58
2	A	True	83–4	89–90
3	B	William Blake	104–6	110–2
4	B	Robert Burns wrote in Scots, English and a combination of both.	53	59
5	B	1958	129	135
6	A	All the national saints' days are celebrated but only in Scotland and Northern Ireland are they official holidays.	85–6	91–2
7	B	Yes, but only in England	159–61	165–7
8	A	Only putting rubbish and recycling out on collection days	159	165
9	B	False	94	100
10	C	1928	138	144
11	B	1999	133–7	139–43
12	B	False	53–5	59–61
13	D	To prevent the further development of slums	64–5	70–1
14	A	True	59–60	65–6
15	D	Every week while Parliament is in session	132	138
16	A	People in the UK are living longer than ever before.	83	89
17	B	Natural knowledge	48	54
18	D	The Queen	125–7	131–3
19	A	The Church of England was restored as the official Church	48	54
	B	The Puritans and Roman Catholics were kept out of power		
20	B	Play jokes on each other	90	96
21	B	False	161	167
22	A	Margaret Thatcher was the UK's first female Prime Minister.	76	82
23	A	Thomas Chippendale was an 18th-century designer of furniture.	103	109
24	A	Stained glass	101	107
	C	Engraving		

PRACTICE TEST 8

1   The Chancellor of the Exchequer is responsible for which area of government policy?

- **A** Immigration
- **B** Education
- **C** Economy
- **D** Health

2   The Scottish Parliament can make laws in which of the following areas?

- **A** Health
- **B** Taxation
- **C** Civil and criminal law
- **D** All of the above

3   The UK is a permanent member of the UN Security Council. How many permanent members does the Security Council have?

- **A** 5
- **B** 15
- **C** 27
- **D** 190

4   The Industrial Revolution saw the rapid growth of which of the following in the 18th and 19th centuries?

- **A** Agriculture
- **B** Democracy
- **C** Population
- **D** Industry

5 **On his escape from the Battle of Worcester,
Charles II famously hid inside what?**

A A forest

B An oak tree

C A cellar

D None of the above

6 **The heptathlon comprises how many different track and field events?**

A 5

B 6

C 7

D 8

7 **Which statement describes 'party politics'
during the reign of William and Mary?**

A There were two main groups, the Liberals and the Conservatives.

B There were two main groups, the Tories and the Whigs.

8 **Which of the following is not the job of the police?**

A To prosecute someone for debt

B To keep the peace

C To prevent and detect crime

D To protect life and property

9 **Is the statement below TRUE or FALSE?**
All Acts of Parliament are made in the name of the Prime Minister.

A True

B False

10 **After the Glorious Revolution, Parliament was still some way from being a democracy. Why?**

   A Only bishops were able to vote

   B Only men who owned property of a certain value could vote

   C Only women were allowed to vote

   D Parliament took control of who could be monarch

11 **Who was king of England at the time of the Norman invasion in 1066?**

   A Herbert

   B Hubert

   C Harold

   D Henry

12 **Which of the following is a line from one of Churchill's famous speeches?**

   A I have a dream

   B The lady's not for turning

   C The only thing we have to fear is fear itself

   D I have nothing to offer but blood, toil, tears and sweat

13 **Which TWO of the following are freedoms offered to citizens and permanent residents of the UK?**

   A Freedom of speech

   B Half day off work on Friday

   C A right to take part in the election of a government

   D Free heating for all

14 **In which city is the Scottish Parliament based?**

   A Sheffield

   B Edinburgh

   C Glasgow

   D Cardiff

15 Which Scottish poet wrote The Bruce about the Battle of Bannockburn?

A Robert Burns

B John Barbour

C Geoffrey Chaucer

D John Milton

16 Which of these statements is not true?

A During Queen Victoria's reign, the middle classes became increasingly significant.

B During Queen Victoria's reign, the size and influence of the British middle class shrank.

17 Rudyard Kipling was awarded which major prize in 1907?

A The Man Booker Prize

B The Pulitzer Prize

C The Nobel Prize in Literature

D The Somerset Maugham Award

18 Who or what were jesters?

A Silver coins of the 18th century

B Combatants on horseback at medieval feasts

C People who told jokes at medieval royal courts

D Men who organised hunts in the Middle Ages

19 Who wrote the poem She Walks in Beauty?

A Sir John Betjeman

B Sir Walter de la Mare

C Elizabeth Browning

D Lord Byron

20 Is the statement below TRUE or FALSE?
The Education Act of 1944 is often called The Butler Act and introduced free secondary education in England and Wales.

- **A** True
- **B** False

21 What are members of the Northern Ireland Parliament known as?

- **A** MPs
- **B** MNIPs
- **C** MLAs
- **D** MEPs

22 Which of these films was directed by David Lean?

- **A** Women in Love
- **B** Four Weddings and a Funeral
- **C** The Killing Fields
- **D** Brief Encounter

23 What is the common name for the Yeoman Warders at the Tower of London?

- **A** Pikestaff
- **B** Queen's Men
- **C** Crown Guards
- **D** Beefeaters

24 Is the statement below TRUE or FALSE?
A mayor is always elected.

- **A** True
- **B** False

ANSWERS: PRACTICE TEST 8

			Handbook reference	Study Guide reference
1	C	Economy	131–2	136–7
2	D	All of the above	133–7	139–43
3	A	5	143	149
4	D	Industry	53–5	59–61
5	B	An oak tree	46–8	52–4
6	C	7	92–3	98–9
7	B	There were two main groups, the Tories and the Whigs.	51	57
8	A	To prosecute someone for debt	145–6	151–2
9	B	False	125–7	131–3
10	B	Only men who owned property of a certain value could vote	51	57
11	C	Harold	33–4	39–40
12	D	I have nothing to offer but blood, toil, tears and sweat	68	74
13	A	Freedom of speech	20–1	26–7
	C	A right to take part in the election of a government		
14	B	Edinburgh	133–7	139–43
15	B	John Barbour	37–9	43–5
16	B	During Queen Victoria's reign, the size and influence of the British middle class shrank.	59	65
17	C	The Nobel Prize in Literature	63	69
18	C	People who told jokes at medieval royal courts	109–10	115–6
19	D	Lord Byron	104–6	110–2
20	A	True	72	78
21	C	MLAs	140–1	146–7
22	D	Brief Encounter	109	115
23	D	Beefeaters	120	126
24	B	False	133	139

PRACTICE TEST 9

1 Which of the following statements is correct?

A The United Nations was set up between the First and Second World Wars.

B The United Nations was set up after the Second World War.

2 What was inscribed on some Iron Age coins?

A Dates

B Values

C Names of Iron Age kings

D Names of Iron Age settlements

3 During the 16th century, which TWO factors predominantly led to a bloody rebellion by the Irish chieftains?

A Extreme poverty and famine

B The imposing of English laws on land inheritance

C High taxes on landowners

D The imposing of Protestantism

4 Henry VIII had six wives. What was the name of his first wife?

A Anne of Cleves

B Catherine Howard

C Catherine of Aragon

D Anne Boleyn

5 The Northern Ireland Assembly was elected in 1999, suspended in 2002 and reinstated in which year?

A 2003

B 2005

C 2007

D 2010

6   Which of these TWO countries did poet and author
     Rudyard Kipling spend time living in?

     A India

     B Japan

     C Fiji

     D USA

7   Is the statement below TRUE or FALSE?
     The Canterbury Tales was one of the first books
     to be printed by William Caxton.

     A True

     B False

8   Acts of Parliament in 1870 and 1882 awarded which right to women?

     A The right to bear arms

     B The right to work

     C The right to attend university

     D The right to keep their own earnings and property after marriage

9   During the early 1970s, Britain admitted 28,000 people of
     Indian origin who had been forced to leave where?

     A The West Indies

     B South Africa

     C China

     D Uganda

10   To go into a betting shop or casino, you have to be what age?

     A 15

     B 16

     C 17

     D 18

11 **Which of these is not a Gilbert and Sullivan comic opera?**

  A The Pirates of Penzance

  B The Mikado

  C A Midsummer Night's Dream

  D HMS Pinafore

12 **William of Normandy invaded England in 1066. Where is Normandy?**

  A Southern Scotland

  B Denmark

  C Northern France

  D Norway

13 **Causing trouble whilst drinking in public can result in which TWO of the following from the police?**

  A An award

  B Arrest

  C A fine

  D Praise

14 **The English Parliament during the reign of Charles I contained many Puritans. What did the Puritans believe in?**

  A Simple and strict religious doctrine and worship

  B Roman Catholic religious doctrine and worship

  C The power of the nobility to control Parliament

  D None of the above

15 **What happens at a polling station or polling place?**

  A The census is collected

  B People vote in elections

  C Taxes are collected

  D People take their driving test

16 Which of the following statements is correct?

A Big Ben refers to the great bell of the clock at the Houses of Parliament.

B Big Ben is a novel written by Sir Kingsley Amis.

17 Around which structure in London is the Remembrance Day service usually held?

A The statue of Eros in Piccadilly Circus

B Nelson's Column in Trafalgar Square

C The London Eye

D The Cenotaph in Whitehall

18 Which of the following statements is correct?

A Dogs in public places must wear a muzzle.

B Dogs in public places must wear a collar showing the owner's name and address.

C Cats in public places must wear a collar.

D All dog owners must have a licence to keep their pets.

19 Is the statement below TRUE or FALSE?
The Welsh Assembly has no power to make laws, but considerable control over public services.

A True

B False

20 Which king annexed Wales to the Crown of England with the Statute of Rhuddlan?

A Charles I

B Harold

C Henry VIII

D Edward I

21 Which of the following statements is correct?

   A Colonists in North America were well educated and interested in ideas of liberty.

   B Colonists in North America were poorly educated and uninterested in politics.

22 Where did Mary Stuart spend most of her childhood?

   A France

   B Germany

   C Spain

   D England

23 The UK has what kind of monarchy?

   A Democratic

   B Constitutional

   C Provisional

   D Absolute

24 Is the statement below TRUE or FALSE?
The candidate who wins the most votes is elected MP for the constituency.

   A True

   B False

ANSWERS: PRACTICE TEST 9

			Handbook reference	Study Guide reference
1	B	The United Nations was set up after the Second World War.	143	149
2	C	Names of Iron Age kings	30–1	36–7
3	B	The imposing of English laws on land inheritance	40–2	46–8
	D	The imposing of Protestantism		
4	C	Catherine of Aragon	41	47
5	C	2007	77	83
6	A	India	63	69
	D	USA		
7	A	True	37–9	43–5
8	D	The right to keep their own earnings and property after marriage	61–2	67–8
9	D	Uganda	73	79
10	D	18	111–2	117–8
11	C	A Midsummer Night's Dream	99–100	105–6
12	C	Northern France	33–4	39–40
13	B	Arrest	144–5	150–1
	C	A fine		
14	A	Simple and strict religious doctrine and worship	46	52
15	B	People vote in elections	139	145
16	A	Big Ben refers to the great bell of the clock at the Houses of Parliament.	113	119
17	D	The Cenotaph in Whitehall	90–1	96–7
18	B	Dogs in public places must wear a collar showing the owner's name and address.	112	118
19	B	False	77	83
20	D	Edward I	35	41
21	A	Colonists in North America were well educated and interested in ideas of liberty.	56	62
22	A	France	43	49
23	B	Constitutional	125	131
24	A	True	130	136

PRACTICE TEST 10

1 **The first farmers probably came to Britain from where?**

- **A** Norway
- **B** South-east Europe
- **C** North America
- **D** North-west Europe

2 **In which of these years did Britain not host the Olympic Games?**

- **A** 1908
- **B** 1928
- **C** 1948
- **D** 2012

3 **How many people make up a Scottish jury?**

- **A** 10
- **B** 12
- **C** 15
- **D** 20

4 **What is a Yorkshire Pudding?**

- **A** A caramel-flavoured dessert
- **B** Meat and potato in a pastry
- **C** Batter cooked in the oven
- **D** Apple and pears with custard

5 **Is the statement below TRUE or FALSE?**
Charles II marched into England with a Scottish army to reclaim his throne.

- **A** True
- **B** False

6   Is the statement below TRUE or FALSE?
*A jump jet capable of taking off and landing vertically
was developed in the UK, and was called the Falcon.*

  A True

  B False

---

7   Is the statement below TRUE or FALSE?
*The Domesday Book no longer exists. It was destroyed
at the end of the Norman Conquest.*

  A True

  B False

---

8   What are MEPs?

  A Members of the English Parliament

  B Members of the European Parliament

  C Modern English parliamentarians

  D Modern European parliamentarians

---

9   Is the statement below TRUE or FALSE?
The MacDonald clan of Glencoe were massacred.

  A True

  B False

**10 The First World War ended in victory for Britain and its allies. At
what exact time and date in 1918 did the war officially end?**

  A 11am on 11 November

  B 10am on 10 October

  C 6am on 6 June

  D 8am on 8 August

11 Is the statement below TRUE or FALSE?
At the beginning of the Middle Ages, England ruled Ireland.

  A True

  B False

12 Which of the following statements is correct?

  A The cabinet's decisions often have to be debated or approved by Parliament.

  B The cabinet's decisions must always be debated or approved by Parliament.

13 Who became queen after the death of Edward VI?

  A His half-sister Mary

  B His wife Mary

  C His cousin Mary

  D Mary, Queen of Scots

14 Which TWO of the following statements are correct?

  A The Romans built roads and public buildings, and created a structure of law.

  B The Romans unified the whole of the British Isles.

  C The Roman army faced no resistance during the invasions.

  D The Romans introduced new plants and animals to Britain.

15 What do you accept and agree to when you become a permanent resident of the UK?

  A Catholic beliefs and values

  B The right to be tried for crimes in your country of origin

  C Traditions of the UK

  D Protestant beliefs and values

16 Is the statement below TRUE or FALSE?
The Home Office selects who becomes a Police and Crime Commissioner (PCC).

   A True

   B False

17 When did Queen Victoria's reign end?

   A 1901

   B 1932

   C 1880

   D 1895

18 How is the electoral register updated?

   A Eligible voters must phone their local councillor

   B Every household receives a registration form, which must be completed and returned

   C Every household must request a registration form

   D Every household receives a phone call to enquire about eligible voters

19 In a Crown Court, who decides the verdict of 'guilty' or 'not guilty'?

   A The defendant

   B The barrister

   C The jury

   D The judge

20 The Archbishop of Canterbury can most accurately be described as what?

   A The spiritual leader of the Church of England

   B The political leader of the Church of England

   C The administrative leader of the Church of England

   D The financial leader of the Church of England

21 What were The Canterbury Tales?

   A A book of Christian doctrine

   B A series of poems

   C A Royal Charter

   D A story about Canterbury Cathedral

22 Which of the following statements is correct?

   A The House of Commons may overrule the House of Lords.

   B The House of Commons may never overrule the House of Lords.

23 Which of the following statements is correct?

   A The UK's constitution is unwritten but includes laws and conventions.

   B The UK's constitution is a single document that includes laws and conventions.

24 Which TWO of the following have the right to vote?

   A Adults who have been granted an indefinite right to remain in the UK

   B UK-born adult citizens

   C Adults who have been given a visa to study in the UK

   D Adults who are naturalised citizens of the UK

ANSWERS: PRACTICE TEST 10

			Handbook reference	Study Guide reference
1	B	South-east Europe	30–1	36–7
2	B	1928	92	98
3	C	15	148	154
4	C	Batter cooked in the oven	108	114
5	A	True	46–8	52–4
6	B	False	74–5	80–1
7	B	False	33–4	39–40
8	B	Members of the European Parliament	130	136
9	A	True	49–50	55–6
10	A	11am on 11 November	64–5	70–1
11	B	False	35	41
12	A	The cabinet's decisions often have to be debated or approved by Parliament.	131–2	137–8
13	A	His half-sister Mary	40–2	46–8
14	A	The Romans built roads and public buildings, and created a structure of law.	31	37
	D	The Romans introduced new plants and animals to Britain.		
15	C	Traditions of the UK	20–1	26–7
16	B	False	145–6	151–2
17	A	1901	59	65
18	B	Every household receives a registration form, which must be completed and returned	138–9	144–5
19	C	The jury	148	154
20	A	The spiritual leader of the Church of England	85	91
21	B	A series of poems	37–9	43–5
22	A	The House of Commons may overrule the House of Lords.	129	135
23	A	The UK's constitution is unwritten but includes laws and conventions.	125	131
24	B	UK-born adult citizens	138	144
	D	Adults who are naturalised citizens of the UK		

PRACTICE TEST 11

1   Where would the Children's Hearings System deal with cases of children or young people accused of an offence?

- **A** Northern Ireland
- **B** Wales
- **C** England
- **D** Scotland

2   Areas of protected countryside that everyone can visit and where people live, work and look after the landscape are called which of the following?

- **A** Greenfield sites
- **B** Country estates
- **C** National parks
- **D** Moorland

3   When did Julius Caesar lead the Roman invasion of Britain?

- **A** 55 BC
- **B** AD 55
- **C** AD 75
- **D** 65 BC

4   What was the Spanish Armada?

- **A** A fleet of Spanish ships
- **B** A Spanish princess
- **C** A treaty with Spain
- **D** The Spanish Army

5 **Is the statement below TRUE or FALSE?**
Dame Judi Dench, Colin Firth and Sir Anthony Hopkins have all won Oscars.

A True

B False

6 **The first people lived in Britain during which period?**

A Ancient times

B The Jurassic period

C The Bronze Age

D The Stone Age

7 **In which language was The Canterbury Tales written?**

A French

B Welsh

C Scottish Gaelic

D English

8 **In England, parliaments were called when the king needed to consult the nobles and for what other reason?**

A To lower taxes

B To create new lords

C To raise money

D To call elections

9 **Near which of these cities is Europe's longest dry ski slope?**

A Aberdeen

B Inverness

C Pitlochrie

D Edinburgh

10 When was the first Union Flag created?

- A 1609
- B 1606
- C 1506
- D 1706

11 At the beginning of the 19th century, which one of the following groups could vote?

- A All adults over the age of 18
- B All women who owned property
- C Property-owning men over the age of 21
- D Property-owning men over the age of 18

12 Lewis Hamilton is a leading figure in which sport?

- A Motor racing
- B Horse racing
- C Tennis
- D Squash

13 Charles II had no legitimate what?

- A Right to the throne
- B Children
- C Government
- D Wife

14 Where can HMS Victory be visited?

- A Southampton
- B Falmouth
- C Poole
- D Portsmouth

15 The Northern Ireland Assembly makes decisions in which TWO of the following areas?

- **A** Agriculture
- **B** Nuclear energy
- **C** Foreign policy
- **D** The environment

16 Which TWO places did the Vikings come from?

- **A** Belgium
- **B** France
- **C** Denmark
- **D** Norway

17 Which TWO facts are true of the individual registration system?

- **A** Registered voters remain on the register until a change in their personal details
- **B** Eligible voters complete their own voter registration forms
- **C** An individual registers his or her whole family to vote
- **D** The electoral register is fully updated each year

18 What did Iron Age people sometimes defend?

- **A** Hill forts
- **B** Castles
- **C** Long walls
- **D** None of the above

19 Which of the following statements is correct?

- **A** You should always introduce yourself to your neighbours when you move into a new house or flat.
- **B** You should never introduce yourself to your new neighbours, but should let them introduce themselves.

20 When did Parliament as we know it today begin to develop?

○ **A** The Iron Age

○ **B** The Stone Age

○ **C** The Middle Ages

○ **D** The Bronze Age

21 Which TWO actions can political parties undertake to gain support for their candidate?

○ **A** Threatening people to make them vote a certain way

○ **B** Handing out leaflets

○ **C** Knocking on doors and talking to people about their candidate

○ **D** Paying people to vote a certain way

22 In the 19th century, the UK became a world-centre for which of the following sectors or industries?

○ **A** Finance

○ **B** Agriculture

○ **C** Wine-making

○ **D** Entertainment

23 Is the statement below TRUE or FALSE?
ISAF is building up the Afghan National Security Forces and helping to create a secure environment in which governance and development can be extended.

○ **A** True

○ **B** False

24 Napoleon fought battles against which TWO of the following?

○ **A** Francis Drake

○ **B** Horatio Nelson

○ **C** The Duke of Wellington

○ **D** Oliver Cromwell

ANSWERS: PRACTICE TEST 11

			Handbook reference	Study Guide reference
1	D	Scotland	149	155
2	C	National parks	112	118
3	A	55 BC	31	37
4	A	A fleet of Spanish ships	43–4	49–50
5	A	True	108–9	114–5
6	D	The Stone Age	30–1	36–7
7	D	English	37–9	43–5
8	C	To raise money	36–7	42–3
9	D	Edinburgh	96	102
10	B	1606	58	64
11	C	Property-owning men over the age of 21	124	130
12	A	Motor racing	96	102
13	B	Children	49	55
14	D	Portsmouth	56–7	62–3
15	A	Agriculture	133–7	139–43
	D	The environment		
16	C	Denmark	33	39
	D	Norway		
17	A	Registered voters remain on the register until a change in their personal details	138–9	144–5
	B	Eligible voters complete their own voter registration forms		
18	A	Hill forts	30–1	36–7
19	A	You should always introduce yourself to your neighbours when you move into a new house or flat.	159	165
20	C	The Middle Ages	36–7	42–3
21	B	Handing out leaflets	161	167
	C	Knocking on doors and talking to people about their candidate		
22	A	Finance	59–60	60–6
23	A	True	77–8	83–4
24	B	Horatio Nelson	56–7	62–3
	C	The Duke of Wellington		

PRACTICE TEST 12

1 Who was William Shakespeare?

- **A** A naval commander
- **B** A Scottish patriot
- **C** An English parliamentarian
- **D** A poet, actor and playwright

2 Which of the following statements is correct?

- **A** The leaders of the Easter uprising were executed under military law.
- **B** The leaders of the Easter uprising were transported to Australia.

3 Charles I believed in, and tried to rule in line with, what principle?

- **A** Democracy
- **B** Communism
- **C** Religious virtue
- **D** The Divine Right of Kings

4 Who is the heir to the throne?

- **A** Prince Philip
- **B** Prince Charles
- **C** The Prime Minister
- **D** All of the above

5 Which of the following statements is correct?

- **A** More than 190 countries belong to NATO.
- **B** More than 190 countries belong to the United Nations.

6 During the First World War, the British fought against countries including Germany, the Ottoman Empire and the Austro-Hungarian Empire. What was this alliance known as?

A The Middle Powers

B The Central Powers

C The Germanic Powers

D The Autocratic Powers

7 Is the statement below TRUE or FALSE?
Breaking a Forced Marriage Protection Order can result in a prison sentence.

A True

B False

8 What is the capital city of Wales?

A Newport

B Cardiff

C Swansea

D Plymouth

9 When did the first farmers come to Britain?

A 10,000 years ago

B 3,000 years ago

C 6,000 years ago

D 8,000 years ago

10 Is the statement below TRUE or FALSE?
During the Industrial Revolution, canals were built to link factories to cities, towns and ports, particularly in the middle and north of England.

A True

B False

11 **Who could not get Parliament to agree to his or her religious and foreign policy views and tried to rule without Parliament?**

- **A** Charles I
- **B** Elizabeth I
- **C** Bloody Mary
- **D** Henry VIII

12 **In the UK, it is acceptable to discriminate against people for which of the following?**

- **A** Age
- **B** Religion or beliefs
- **C** Pregnancy or maternity
- **D** None of the above

13 **During the reign of which king of England was the Domesday Book compiled?**

- **A** Harold
- **B** William the Conqueror
- **C** Kenneth MacAlpin
- **D** Alfred the Great

14 **Which TWO of the following deal with civil disputes?**

- **A** Sheriff Court
- **B** Crown Court
- **C** County Court
- **D** Youth Court

15 **Which of the following is a core value of the civil service?**

- **A** Laziness
- **B** Party loyalty
- **C** Integrity
- **D** Bribery

16 A vehicle more than three years old must pass an MOT test every year. What does MOT stand for?

  A Maintenance of Transportation

  B Migrant Order for Transport

  C Motor-vehicle Optimisation Test

  D Ministry of Transport

17 Is the statement below TRUE or FALSE?
King Henry I was on the throne at the time of the Magna Carta.

  A True

  B False

18 Who was Kenneth MacAlpin?

  A A Danish king

  B An Anglo-Saxon king

  C A Scottish king

  D A Viking

19 Which country are Loch Lomond and the Trossachs National Park found?

  A Wales

  B England

  C Scotland

  D Northern Ireland

20 A poll card includes which TWO pieces of information?

  A The date of the election

  B Who you should vote for

  C Where the polling station or polling place is located

  D How much tax you should pay

21 West Germany, France, Luxembourg, the Netherlands and Italy formed the European Economic Community (EEC) in 1957 along with which other country?

- **A** Ireland
- **B** Belgium
- **C** Sweden
- **D** Albania

22 In Northern Ireland, children who have committed an offence are dealt with by which of the following?

- **A** A Sheriff Court
- **B** A Crown Court
- **C** The Children's Hearings System
- **D** A system of youth conferencing

23 The first day of one notorious battle in 1916 resulted in 60,000 British casualties. What was this battle?

- **A** The Battle of the Somme
- **B** The Battle of the Bulge
- **C** The Battle of Agincourt
- **D** The Battle of the River Plate

24 What happened to Catherine Parr soon after she remarried, following the death of Henry VIII?

- **A** She had a son
- **B** She died
- **C** She had a daughter
- **D** She was executed

ANSWERS: PRACTICE TEST 12

			Handbook reference	Study Guide reference
1	D	A poet, actor and playwright	44	50
2	A	The leaders of the Easter uprising were executed under military law.	65–6	71–2
3	D	The Divine Right of Kings	45–6	51–2
4	B	Prince Charles	125–7	131–3
5	B	More than 190 countries belong to the United Nations.	143	149
6	B	The Central Powers	64–5	70–1
7	A	True	155	161
8	B	Cardiff	81	87
9	C	6,000 years ago	30–1	36–7
10	A	True	53–5	59–61
11	A	Charles I	45–6	51–2
12	D	None of the above	154	160
13	B	William the Conqueror	33–4	39–40
14	A	Sheriff Court	151	157
	C	County Court		
15	C	Integrity	133	139
16	D	Ministry of Transport	157	163
17	B	False	36–7	42–3
18	C	A Scottish king	33	39
19	C	Scotland	117	123
20	A	The date of the election	139	145
	C	Where the polling station or polling place is located		
21	B	Belgium	76	82
22	D	A system of youth conferencing	149	155
23	A	The Battle of the Somme	64–5	70–1
24	B	She died	41	47

PRACTICE TEST 13

1 **Is the statement below TRUE or FALSE?**
Following the abolition of slavery, two million Chinese and Indian workers were employed to replace the freed slaves.

A True

B False

2 **How many members does a jury have in England?**

A 10

B 12

C 15

D 20

3 **Mary Stuart, the queen of Scotland, was often known by which other name?**

A Mary Tudor

B Bloody Mary

C Mary, Queen of the Highlands

D Mary, Queen of Scots

4 **Gertrude Jekyll is famous for her designs in which field?**

A Fashion

B Gardening

C Silverware

D Pottery

5 **Which of these statements about Roald Dahl is not true?**

A He began to publish books and short stories in the 1940s

B He served in the Royal Air Force during the Second World War

C He had Norwegian parents

D He served in the Royal Navy during the Second World War

6 **Which of the following statements is correct?**

A In Scotland, serious offences are tried in a Sheriff Court.

B In Scotland, serious offences are tried in a Crown Court.

7 **During 1940, German troops defeated allied forces whilst advancing through which country?**

A Russia

B France

C Greece

D Argentina

8 **In which TWO places are arrangements different for taking your Life in the UK Test?**

A Scotland

B Ireland

C Isle of Man

D Channel Islands

9 **Which of the following was a co-discoverer of insulin?**

A John Logie Baird

B Sir Frank Whittle

C John MacLeod

D Sir Robert Watson-Watt

10 **Is the statement below TRUE or FALSE?**
The whole British Empire was involved in the First World War, with troops from India, the West Indies, Africa, and Australia all fighting on behalf of the British.

A True

B False

11 **The Victorian period famously saw reformers leading moves to improve conditions for which section of society?**

- **A** The aristocracy
- **B** The poor
- **C** The middle classes
- **D** The clergy

12 **During which king's reign in 1665 was there a major outbreak of plague in London?**

- **A** Charles II
- **B** James I
- **C** James II
- **D** Charles I

13 **What were women campaigning for the right to vote known as?**

- **A** Suffragettes
- **B** Votettes
- **C** Democrettes
- **D** Feminettes

14 **In Scotland, the legal system developed differently from the one in England in that its laws were 'codified'. What is meant by codified?**

- **A** Less complicated
- **B** Dictated by Parliament
- **C** Written down
- **D** Based on tradition

15 **Is the statement below TRUE or FALSE?**
Charles I was interested in science. During his reign, the 'Royal Society' was formed.

- **A** True
- **B** False

16 **Which TWO of these careers did Winston Churchill follow before becoming a Conservative MP in 1900?**

A Teacher

B Vicar

C Journalist

D Soldier

17 **What did the missionaries teach the Anglo-Saxons?**

A About other cultures

B About Christianity

C About other languages

D About trade

18 **Which of the following statements is correct?**

A James I and Charles I were very skilled at negotiating with Parliament.

B James I and Charles I believed in the 'Divine Right of Kings' and that they could rule without the approval of Parliament

19 **Is the statement below TRUE or FALSE?**
The symbol of the House of Lancaster was a red rose and the symbol of the House of York was a white rose.

A True

B False

20 **Who wrote Paradise Lost?**

A William Shakespeare

B Salman Rushdie

C Rider Haggard

D John Milton

21 The Festival of Lights is another name for which of the following?

- **A** Vaisakhi
- **B** Hannukah
- **C** Diwali
- **D** Eid ul Adha

22 Who gave the throne to her Protestant son, James VI?

- **A** Elizabeth I
- **B** Mary Tudor
- **C** Mary, Queen of Scots
- **D** Bloody Mary

23 The game of golf is traditionally thought to have originated in which country?

- **A** England
- **B** Spain
- **C** USA
- **D** Scotland

24 Is the statement below TRUE or FALSE?
The Royal Society is the oldest surviving scientific society in the world.

- **A** True
- **B** False

ANSWERS: PRACTICE TEST 13

			Handbook reference	Study Guide reference
1	A	True	55–6	61–2
2	B	12	148	154
3	D	Mary, Queen of Scots	43	49
4	B	Gardening	102–3	108–9
5	D	He served in the Royal Navy during the Second World War	77	83
6	A	In Scotland, serious offences are tried in a Sheriff Court.	148	154
7	B	France	66–9	72–5
8	C	Isle of Man	22–3	27–9
	D	Channel Islands		
9	C	John MacLeod	74–5	80–1
10	A	True	64–5	70–1
11	B	The poor	59	65
12	A	Charles II	48	54
13	A	Suffragettes	61–2	67–8
14	C	Written down	36–7	42–3
15	B	False	48	54
16	C	Journalist	68	74
	D	Soldier		
17	B	About Christianity	31–3	37–9
18	B	James I and Charles I believed in the 'Divine Right of Kings' and that they could rule without the approval of Parliament	45–6	51–2
19	A	True	39	45
20	D	John Milton	104–6	110–2
21	C	Diwali	88	94
22	C	Mary, Queen of Scots	43	49
23	D	Scotland	95	101
24	A	True	48	54

PRACTICE TEST 14

1 Which one of the following is not a benefit of volunteering?

- **A** Being able to add new experience to your CV
- **B** Being paid
- **C** Having a chance to practise English
- **D** Meeting new people

2 What did hereditary peers lose in 1999?

- **A** The right to own land
- **B** The automatic right to sit in the House of Lords
- **C** The right to elect other peers to the House of Lords
- **D** The right to speak in Parliament

3 Jane Seymour gave birth to the son Henry VIII wanted. What was his name?

- **A** Henry
- **B** Edmund
- **C** Edward
- **D** Richard

4 If you can't make it to a polling station to vote, you can register for which of the following?

- **A** A postal ballot
- **B** An absentee ballot
- **C** An absentee vote
- **D** A virtual ballot

5   Is the sentence below TRUE or FALSE?
Al Qa'ida is the only terrorist threat to the UK.

   A True

   B False

6   Is this statement TRUE or FALSE?
During Queen Victoria's reign, the French Empire became the largest Empire the world has ever seen.

   A True

   B False

7   Who decides what should happen in legal disputes over contracts, property rights or employment rights?

   A The media

   B The police

   C The judiciary

   D The peers

8   During the 18th century, Britain fought a number of wars with which country?

   A India

   B South Africa

   C Spain

   D France

9   Which of the following statements is correct?

   A The National Assembly for Wales and the Welsh government are based in Edinburgh.

   B The National Assembly for Wales and the Welsh government are based in Cardiff.

10 **Which of the following statements is correct?**

    A The Commonwealth is a group of countries that support each other and work together.

    B The Commonwealth is a group of regions that together make up a federal republic.

11 **Is the statement below TRUE or FALSE?**
Mo Farah was the first person to sail around the world single-handed.

    A True

    B False

12 **What sorts of stories were depicted in the stained glass windows of many cathedrals built in the Middle Ages?**

    A Stories about kings and coronations

    B Stories about battles and victories

    C Stories about the Bible and saints

    D Stories about communities and farming

13 **Is the statement below TRUE or FALSE?**
St Columba became the first Archbishop of Canterbury.

    A True

    B False

14 **Is the statement below TRUE or FALSE?**
Sake Dean Mahomet was born in 1759 and grew up in the Bengal region of India.

    A True

    B False

15 **Which of these countries was part of the British Empire during Victoria's reign?**

- **A** France
- **B** Switzerland
- **C** USA
- **D** India

16 **Which organisation was founded in 1895 and now has over 61,000 volunteers helping to preserve important buildings, the countryside and the coastline?**

- **A** The National Trust
- **B** The Countryside Alliance
- **C** Country Landowners Association
- **D** The National Gardens Scheme

17 **Which of the following statements is correct?**

- **A** In 1789 there was an unpopular new government in France and Britain declared war.
- **B** In 1789 there was a revolution in France and the new French government declared war on Britain.

18 **During the reign of Henry VII, what happened to the power of the nobility in England?**

- **A** It was reduced
- **B** It increased
- **C** It was abolished
- **D** It was absolute

19 **Is the statement below TRUE or FALSE?**
The Old Bailey is one of the world's most famous Magistrates' Courts.

- **A** True
- **B** False

20 During the 19th century, Britain and the East India Company gained control of large parts of which TWO countries?

- **A** The United States
- **B** Canada
- **C** India
- **D** Singapore

21 Is the statement below TRUE or FALSE?
The Hundred Years War between England and France lasted 99 years.

- **A** True
- **B** False

22 Is the statement below TRUE or FALSE?
Briton Sir Tim Berners-Lee invented the World Wide Web and it was successfully used for the first time on 25 December 1990.

- **A** True
- **B** False

23 Is the statement below TRUE or FALSE?
Britain had colonies in southern Africa in the 19th century.

- **A** True
- **B** False

24 Which famous religious building has been the coronation church since 1066 and is the final resting place for 17 monarchs?

- **A** Westminster Abbey
- **B** York Minster
- **C** St Paul's Cathedral
- **D** Westminster Cathedral

ANSWERS: PRACTICE TEST 14

			Handbook reference	Study Guide reference
1	B	Being paid	162–4	168–70
2	B	The automatic right to sit in the House of Lords	129	135
3	C	Edward	41	47
4	A	A postal ballot	139	145
5	B	False	147	153
6	B	False	59	65
7	C	The judiciary	148	154
8	D	France	56	62
9	B	The National Assembly for Wales and the Welsh government are based in Cardiff.	133–7	139–43
10	A	The Commonwealth is a group of countries that support each other and work together.	141	147
11	B	False	92–3	98–9
12	C	Stories about the Bible and saints	37–9	43–5
13	B	False	31–3	37–9
14	A	True	55	61
15	D	India	59	65
16	A	The National Trust	112	118
17	B	In 1789 there was a revolution in France and the new French government declared war on Britain.	56–7	62–3
18	A	It was reduced	40–2	46–8
19	B	False	149	155
20	B	Canada	53–5	59–61
	C	India		
21	B	False	35	41
22	A	True	74–5	80–1
23	A	True	53–5	59–61
24	A	Westminster Abbey	85–6	91–2

PRACTICE TEST 15

1 During the 19th century, which sector of the Irish economy supported around two-thirds of its people?

A Tourism

B Farming

C Manufacturing

D Shipbuilding

2 What do we know about the life of Anne Boleyn?

A She had one daughter with Henry VIII named Elizabeth

B She never married

C She married Henry VIII late in his life, and survived him

D She ruled with William III after the Glorious Revolution

3 Which TWO of the following factors contributed to the Industrial Revolution in Britain?

A The foundation of the modern welfare state

B The development of steam power and machinery

C The outbreak of plague

D The repealing of the Corn Laws

4 Which of the following statements is correct?

A The Beveridge Report of 1942 outlined a plan to end the war in Europe.

B The Beveridge Report of 1942 provided the basis of the modern welfare state.

5 **By 1200, the English ruled an area of Ireland around Dublin known as what?**

- **A** The Pate
- **B** The Pict
- **C** The Pale
- **D** The Plain

6 **Official reports of parliamentary proceeding are published in which of the following?**

- **A** The BBC magazine
- **B** Hansard
- **C** The Telegraph
- **D** The Sunday Times

7 **Which of these sectors was not nationalised by the post-war Labour government?**

- **A** Coal mining
- **B** The railways
- **C** Gas, electric and water supplies
- **D** Farming

8 **James II invaded Ireland in an attempt to regain the throne with an army from which country?**

- **A** Germany
- **B** France
- **C** Scotland
- **D** Wales

9 **Which of these statements is correct?**

- **A** You will need the help of a lawyer to issue a small claim.
- **B** You do not need the help of a lawyer to issue a small claim.

10 Following the introduction of the Bill of Rights, monarchs were required to ask Parliament to renew funding for which TWO of the following each year?

- **A** Army
- **B** Building of castles
- **C** Palaces
- **D** Navy

11 Why were more castles built in Britain and Ireland in the Middle Ages?

- **A** They were cheap to build
- **B** They were defensive strongholds
- **C** They were status symbols for the nobility
- **D** They created work for tradesmen

12 Which of the following statements is correct?

- **A** 11 November commemorates soldiers who died in World War One as well as those who have died in all conflicts involving the UK since then.
- **B** 11 November only commemorates soldiers who died in World War One.

13 Is this statement TRUE or FALSE?
In Wales and Northern Ireland, the established Churches are respectively the Church of Wales and the Church of Ulster.

- **A** True
- **B** False

14 Is the statement below TRUE or FALSE?
The BBC began the world's first regular television service in 1936.

- **A** True
- **B** False

15 **Is the statement below TRUE or FALSE?**
The Archbishop of Canterbury opens the parliamentary session each year.

A True

B False

16 **Which artist is considered to be the one who raised the profile of landscape painting?**

A John Constable

B Thomas Gainsborough

C David Allan

D Joseph Turner

17 **Which TWO of these books were written by Rudyard Kipling?**

A Just So Stories

B The Jungle Book

C The Time Machine

D Animal Farm

18 **Which of the following is a famous tennis tournament played in the UK every year?**

A Wimbledon

B The Grand National

C The Open

D Six Nations

19 **Which of the following statements is correct?**

A Margaret Thatcher was the longest-serving Prime Minister of the UK in the 20th century.

B Margaret Thatcher was the second longest-serving Prime Minister of the UK in the 20th century.

20 What happened when Charles I tried to impose a revised Prayer Book onto the Presbyterian Church in Scotland?

- **A** The Scottish rebelled and formed an army
- **B** It was very popular across the Union
- **C** It was accepted after some amendments
- **D** The Pope came to England to help Charles I

21 Can young people in every part of the UK volunteer with the National Citizen Service?

- **A** Yes, but each part of the UK has a different website for information about the service
- **B** No, only young people resident in England can volunteer

22 St George is the patron saint of which UK country?

- **A** England
- **B** Scotland
- **C** Wales
- **D** Northern Ireland

23 Is the statement below TRUE or FALSE?
The American colonies rebelled against the British Parliament in the 18th century because they didn't want to pay taxes without representation in Parliament.

- **A** True
- **B** False

24 Which of the following countries does not belong to the Commonwealth?

- **A** Canada
- **B** Germany
- **C** Ghana
- **D** Singapore

ANSWERS: PRACTICE TEST 15

			Handbook reference	Study Guide reference
1	B	Farming	61	67
2	A	She had one daughter with Henry VIII named Elizabeth	41	47
3	B	The development of steam power and machinery	53	59
	D	The repealing of the Corn Laws		
4	B	The Beveridge Report of 1942 provided the basis of the modern welfare state.	71	77
5	C	The Pale	35	41
6	B	Hansard	137	143
7	D	Farming	70–1	76–7
8	B	France	49	55
9	B	You do not need the help of a lawyer to issue a small claim.	151	157
10	A	Army	51	57
	D	Navy		
11	B	They were defensive strongholds	37–9	43–5
12	A	11 November commemorates soldiers who died in World War One as well as those who have died in all conflicts involving the UK since then.	90	96
13	B	False	85	91
14	A	True	66	72
15	B	False	125–7	131–3
16	D	Joseph Turner	101	107
17	A	Just So Stories	63	69
	B	The Jungle Book		
18	A	Wimbledon	96	102
19	A	Margaret Thatcher was the longest-serving Prime Minister of the UK in the 20th century.	76	82
20	A	The Scottish rebelled and formed an army	46	52
21	A	Yes, but each part of the UK has a different website for information about the service	162–4	168–70
22	A	England	85–6	91–2
23	A	True	56	62
24	B	Germany	141–2	147–8

PRACTICE TEST 16

1   Some people in Britain were opposed to the slave trade. Who set up the first formal anti-slavery groups in the late 1700s?

- **A** Methodists
- **B** Mormons
- **C** Quakers
- **D** Puritans

2   What is the capital city of Scotland?

- **A** Edinburgh
- **B** Glasgow
- **C** Dundee
- **D** Aberdeen

3   The Elizabethan period in England was a time of growing patriotism. What do we mean by this?

- **A** There was unrest and instability
- **B** The monarchy became unpopular
- **C** The country became more democratic
- **D** A feeling of pride in being English

4   On which day do people send cards to someone they admire, anonymously?

- **A** Christmas Day
- **B** New Year's Day
- **C** Valentine's Day
- **D** April Fool's Day

5   As well as giving legal advice, solicitors are able to do which TWO of the following?

A Represent clients in court

B Arrest suspects

C Take action for a client

D Change the law

6   How many countries belong to the Commonwealth?

A 12

B 25

C 39

D 54

7   Which of the following statements is correct?

A During the Elizabethan period, English settlers began to colonise America.

B During the Elizabethan period, English settlers began to colonise Australia.

8   Which of the following is a document or piece of legislation that sets out fundamental rights or freedoms?

A The UK Constitution

B The Habeas Corpus Act

C The Statute of Rhuddlan

D The Act of Union

9   Is the statement below TRUE or FALSE?
Henry VIII continued his father's work to centralise the administrative powers of England.

A True

B False

10 In which part of the UK was pioneering doctor Alexander Fleming born in 1881?

    A Wales

    B Scotland

    C East Anglia

    D Cornwall

11 Which of the following statements is correct?

    A At its peak, the British Empire had an estimated population of just under 400 million.

    B At its peak, the British Empire had an estimated population of just under 40 million.

12 In 1913, the British government promised Home Rule for Ireland. Which group within Ireland threatened to resist this move by force?

    A The Protestants in the south

    B The Muslims in the east

    C The Buddhists in the west

    D The Protestants in the north

13 Is the statement below TRUE or FALSE?
In 1688, Protestant leaders in England asked William of Orange to invade England and proclaim himself king.

    A True

    B False

14 Is the statement below TRUE or FALSE?
All MPs represent one of the main political parties.

    A True

    B False

15 Who were the Picts?

A Ancestors of the Irish people

B Ancestors of the Welsh people

C Ancestors of the Scottish people

D Ancestors of the English people

16 At which of the following famous UK landmarks would you find biomes?

A Giant's Causeway

B The Eden Project

C Snowdonia

D Edinburgh Castle

17 During the English Civil War, in which TWO battles was Charles I's army defeated?

A Battle of Bosworth Field

B Battle of Naseby

C Battle of Marston Moor

D Battle of Hastings

18 Why did Henry VIII marry Anne of Cleves?

A For political reasons

B He loved her

C To have a male heir

D She was beautiful

19 Anyone who wishes to buy tobacco or tobacco products must be over what age?

A 14

B 16

C 18

D 21

20 **Which Northern Irish portrait artist, who died in 1941, painted some portraits of the Royal Family?**

- **A** Sir John Lavery
- **B** Paul Henry
- **C** Basil Blackshaw
- **D** Markey Robinson

21 **Is the statement below TRUE or FALSE?**
Charles II was crowned king of England, Wales, Scotland and Ireland in the Restoration after the English Civil War.

- **A** True
- **B** False

22 **After Protestants, which is the biggest denomination of Christianity in the UK?**

- **A** Jehovah's Witnesses
- **B** Roman Catholic
- **C** Ethiopian Orthodox
- **D** Christian Science

23 **Who introduced a system called feudalism to Britain?**

- **A** Vikings
- **B** Jutes
- **C** Normans
- **D** Anglo-Saxons

24 **Pumpkins, lit with candles, are used to celebrate which tradition?**

- **A** Bonfire Night
- **B** Halloween
- **C** Midsummer
- **D** May Day

ANSWERS: PRACTICE TEST 16

			Handbook reference	Study Guide reference
1	C	Quakers	55–6	61–2
2	A	Edinburgh	81	87
3	D	A feeling of pride in being English.	43–4	49–50
4	C	Valentine's Day	90	96
5	A	Represent clients in court	152–3	158–9
	C	Take action for a client		
6	D	54	141–2	147–8
7	A	During the Elizabethan period, English settlers began to colonise America.	43–4	49–50
8	B	The Habeas Corpus Act	153–4	159–60
9	A	True	40–2	46–8
10	B	Scotland	70	76
11	A	At its peak, the British Empire had an estimated population of just under 400 million.	59	65
12	D	The Protestants in the north	65–6	71–2
13	A	True	49–50	55–6
14	B	False	132	138
15	C	Ancestors of the Scottish people	31	37
16	B	The Eden Project	114	120
17	B	Battle of Naseby	46–8	52–4
	C	Battle of Marston Moor		
18	A	For political reasons	41	47
19	C	18	144–5	150–1
20	A	Sir John Lavery	101	107
21	A	True	48	54
22	B	Roman Catholic	84–5	90–1
23	C	Normans	35–6	41–2
24	B	Halloween	90	96

PRACTICE TEST 17

1   When William of Orange came to the throne with his wife Mary, this later became known as the Glorious Revolution. Why?

- **A** It signalled the start of the Hundred Years War
- **B** William of Orange defeated a much larger army
- **C** It led to the Reformation and the formation of the Protestant Church
- **D** There was no fighting in England

2   Which of the following statements is correct?

- **A** During the reign of Charles I, Parliament attempted to take control of the English army following a rebellion in Ireland.
- **B** During the reign of Charles I, Irish Catholics supported the views of the Puritans.

3   Which political party was Clement Attlee a member of?

- **A** Liberal Democrats
- **B** Conservative
- **C** Green
- **D** Labour

4   A conflict in which of these areas in the 1990s involved British troops?

- **A** The Maldives
- **B** The former Republic of Yugoslavia
- **C** The Baltic states
- **D** Lapland

5   Is the statement below TRUE or FALSE?
There are no differences between the court systems of England, Northern Ireland, Scotland and Wales.

  A True

  B False

6   Which of the following statements is correct?

  A By 1400, in England, official documents were being written in English and English was the preferred language of Parliament and the royal court.

  B By 1400, a mixture of Norman French and Anglo-Saxon was being spoken and no unified language was emerging.

7   George and Robert Stephenson are famous for pioneering what?

  A The railway engine

  B The aeroplane

  C The telephone

  D The electric light bulb

8   Is the statement below TRUE or FALSE?
Protestants believed that a person's own relationship with God was more important than submitting to the authority of the Church.

  A True

  B False

9   Which of the following statements is correct?

  A Completed ballots must be handed to an election official.

  B Completed ballots must be placed in a ballot box.

10 **Which TWO of the following are British inventions?**

A Jet engine

B Helicopter

C Golf cart

D Hovercraft

11 **Is the statement below TRUE or FALSE?**
In the UK, everybody has the right to choose their religion or choose not to practise a religion.

A True

B False

12 **Is the statement below TRUE or FALSE?**
The language of the Iron Age was part of the Celtic language family.

A True

B False

13 **When England became a republic, after Charles I lost the English Civil War, it no longer had what?**

A A parliament

B A National anthem

C A monarch

D A Prime Minister

14 **Is the statement below TRUE or FALSE?**
In 1690, following his unsuccessful attempt to regain his throne in Ireland, James II fled back to the Netherlands.

A True

B False

15 Income tax is not paid on which of the following forms of income?

  A Pension

  B Money you win on the lottery

  C Benefits

  D All of the above

16 Which of the following statements is correct?

  A The small claims procedure is an informal way of helping people who have been victims of identity theft or fraud.

  B The small claims procedure is an informal way of helping people settle minor disputes without needing a lawyer.

17 Which of the following is a British invention or innovation?

  A A Turing machine

  B Micro Machines

  C The telephone

  D The photocopier

18 Is the statement below TRUE or FALSE?
It is possible to find information about visiting Parliament on the UK Parliament website.

  A True

  B False

19 Is the statement below TRUE or FALSE?
The Houses of Parliament are built in the medieval 'gothic' style of architecture.

  A True

  B False

20 The Elizabeth Tower is part of which building in London?

A St Paul's Cathedral

B Houses of Parliament

C Mansion House

D Buckingham Palace

21 Is it possible for the leader of the opposition to become Prime Minister?

A Yes, if the Prime Minister resigns

B Yes, if his or her party wins a General Election

22 People usually spend Christmas Day at home and enjoy a special meal that normally includes Christmas pudding, mince pies and which meat?

A Duck

B Turkey

C Guinea fowl

D Pork

23 Which TWO of the following describe the purpose of the UN Security Council?

A To promote human rights

B To recommend action during an international crisis

C To recommend action where there is a threat to peace

D To make international law

24 Which Acts of Parliament, passed in 1832 and 1867, abolished rotten boroughs, gave more parliamentary seats to urban areas and greatly increased the right of people to vote?

A The Change Acts

B The Voting Acts

C The Election Acts

D The Reform Acts

ANSWERS: PRACTICE TEST 17

			Handbook reference	Study Guide reference
1	D	There was no fighting in England	49–50	55–6
2	A	During the reign of Charles I, Parliament attempted to take control of the English army following a rebellion in Ireland.	46	52
3	D	Labour	71	77
4	B	The former Republic of Yugoslavia	77–8	83–4
5	B	False	148	154
6	A	By 1400, in England, official documents were being written in English and English was the preferred language of Parliament and the royal court.	37–9	43–5
7	A	The railway engine	59–60	65–6
8	A	True	40–2	46–8
9	B	Completed ballots must be placed in a ballot box.	139	145
10	A	Jet engine	74–5	80–1
	D	Hovercraft		
11	A	True	84	90
12	A	True	30–1	36–7
13	C	Monarch	46–8	52–4
14	B	False	49–50	55–6
15	B	Money you win on the lottery	155–6	161–2
16	B	The small claims procedure is an informal way of helping people settle minor disputes without needing a lawyer.	151	157
17	A	A Turing machine	74–5	80–1
18	A	True	140–1	146–7
19	A	True	102–3	108–9
20	B	Houses of Parliament	113	119
21	B	Yes, if his or her party wins a General Election	132	138
22	B	Turkey	87	93
23	B	To recommend action during an international crisis	143	149
	C	To recommend action where there is a threat to peace		
24	D	The Reform Acts	61–2	67–8

PRACTICE TEST 18

1   Police forces are headed by whom?

  A Ministers

  B Generals

  C Mayors

  D Chief Constables

2   Is the statement below TRUE or FALSE?
A Formula 1 Grand Prix race is held in Britain every year.

  A True

  B False

3   Is the statement below TRUE or FALSE?
Many colonists had gone to North America in order to have religious freedom.

  A True

  B False

4   During the 1960s, Parliament passed new laws that made it illegal for employers to discriminate against women because of their gender and gave them which right?

  A Free lunches

  B Equal pay

  C Childcare at work

  D Two years' maternity leave

5   Who wrote the piece of music, Balthazar's Feast?

  A Henry Purcell

  B Sir William Walton

  C Gustav Holst

  D Sir Edward Elgar

6 **Is the statement below TRUE or FALSE?**
The 1950s were a time of serious unrest in Northern Ireland.

  A True

  B False

7 **The UK joined which international organisation in 1973?**

  A The UN

  B NATO

  C The Commonwealth

  D The European Union

8 **Mary Stuart was forced to flee England after being accused of murder. Who was she accused of murdering?**

  A Her father

  B Her husband

  C Her brother

  D Her sister

9 **Which of these countries did not fight on the side of the Allied Powers during the First World War?**

  A Bulgaria

  B Italy

  C USA

  D Serbia

10 **King Edward I of England annexed Wales to the crown of England by which statute?**

  A The Statute of Caernarfon

  B The Statute of Gwynedd

  C The Statute of Carmarthen

  D The Statute of Rhuddlan

11   Where in London is the White Tower?

- **A** Tower of London
- **B** Buckingham Palace
- **C** Palace of Westminster
- **D** St Paul's Cathedral

12   Is the statement below TRUE or FALSE?
The Reformation failed in Scotland and the country remained strongly Catholic.

- **A** True
- **B** False

13   How did Jane Seymour die?

- **A** Following childbirth
- **B** She was executed
- **C** Old age
- **D** The plague

14   Who won the English Civil War in 1646?

- **A** Parliament
- **B** The Cavaliers
- **C** The king
- **D** None of the above

15   What special type of windows did many cathedrals built in the Middle Ages have?

- **A** Arched
- **B** Mullioned
- **C** Stained glass
- **D** Sash

16 Which of the following statements is correct?

- **A** Countries are obliged to belong to the Commonwealth.
- **B** Countries join the Commonwealth voluntarily.

17 Which TWO of the following names may be given to the day before Lent starts?

- **A** Ash Wednesday
- **B** Shrove Tuesday
- **C** Good Friday
- **D** Pancake Day

18 Sir Chris Hoy is a famous sportsman in which event or sport?

- **A** Athletics
- **B** Ice skating
- **C** Swimming
- **D** Cycling

19 Which English king led his army to victory at the Battle of Agincourt?

- **A** Henry V
- **B** Henry VII
- **C** Henry II
- **D** Henry VIII

20 During the 17th century, many people left Britain and Ireland to settle in which of the following places?

- **A** France
- **B** Africa
- **C** America
- **D** London

PRACTICE TEST 18

21 Is the statement below TRUE or FALSE?
It is legal to carry a weapon if it is for self-defence.

A True

B False

22 There was growth in British film, fashion and music during the 1960s. Which TWO of these were very popular sixties British pop groups?

A Abba

B The Beatles

C The Rolling Stones

D The Beach Boys

23 The four shortlisted works for the Turner Prize are shown at which London venue?

A British Museum

B Tate Britain

C National Gallery

D Victoria and Albert Museum

24 Fighting broke out between colonists in North America and British forces in the late 18th century. What did 13 colonies declare in 1776?

A Defeat

B Surrender

C Independence

D An alliance

ANSWERS: PRACTICE TEST 18

			Handbook reference	Study Guide reference
1	D	Chief Constables	145–6	151–2
2	A	True	96	102
3	A	True	56	62
4	B	Equal pay	73	79
5	B	Sir William Walton	97–9	104
6	B	False	75	81
7	D	The European Union	142	148
8	B	Her husband	43	49
9	A	Bulgaria	64–5	70–1
10	D	The Statute of Rhuddlan	35	41
11	A	Tower of London	102–3	108–9
12	B	False	43	49
13	A	Following childbirth	41	47
14	A	Parliament	46–8	52–4
15	C	Stained glass	37–9	43–5
16	B	Countries join the Commonwealth voluntarily.	141–2	147–8
17	B	Shrove Tuesday	88	94
	D	Pancake Day		
18	D	Cycling	92–3	98–9
19	A	Henry V	35	41
20	C	America	52	58
21	B	False	144–5	150–1
22	B	The Beatles	73	79
	C	The Rolling Stones		
23	B	Tate Britain	100–1	106–7
24	C	Independence	56	62

PRACTICE TEST 19

1 Who was Cnut (Canute)?

- **A** A Danish king of England
- **B** An Anglo-Saxon king of England
- **C** A Scottish lord
- **D** A Viking warrior

2 Who is not appointed to the cabinet?

- **A** The Chancellor of the Exchequer
- **B** The Speaker
- **C** The Foreign Secretary
- **D** The Home Secretary

3 Scotland developed its own Parliament. This was divided into three parts. What were they called?

- **A** The lords, the commons and the clergy
- **B** The lords, the commons and the Estates
- **C** The lords, the commons and the Houses
- **D** The lords, the commons and the bishops

4 Is the statement below TRUE or FALSE?
English laws and the English language were introduced to Wales during the Middle Ages.

- **A** True
- **B** False

5 Is the statement below TRUE or FALSE?
The Council of Europe is another name for the European Union.

- **A** True
- **B** False

6   Which of the following is the title of the David Lean directed film of 1962?

   A Lawrence of Asia

   B Lawrence of Australia

   C Lawrence of Amsterdam

   D Lawrence of Arabia

7   Looking after the environment involves which TWO of the following?

   A Buying new products whenever possible

   B Buying recycled products whenever possible

   C Recycling waste when possible

   D Using more energy when possible

8   It is enshrined in law that men and women in the UK have equal rights to work, own property, marry and which of the following?

   A Divorce

   B Cook meals

   C Travel abroad

   D Own a dog

9   The Scottish Parliament has how many members?

   A 60

   B 108

   C 129

   D 360

10   Who were the Jutes, Angles and Saxons?

   A Tribespeople from Northern Europe

   B Romans

   C Tribespeople from Wales

   D Tribespeople from Scotland

11 **Which country's coastline did James Cook map, leading to the establishment of colonies there?**

- **A** Indonesia
- **B** Portugal
- **C** South Africa
- **D** Australia

12 **About which conflict did poets Wilfred Owen and Siegfried Sassoon write?**

- **A** Crimean War
- **B** Boer War
- **C** First World War
- **D** Second World War

13 **Which Jewish religious festival happens in November or December every year?**

- **A** Eid al-Fitr
- **B** Eid ul Adha
- **C** Hannukah
- **D** Vaisakhi

14 **The 'Ashes' are played for between England and Australia in which sport?**

- **A** Rugby union
- **B** Tennis
- **C** Darts
- **D** Cricket

15 **Which of the following statements is correct?**

- **A** Mary, Queen of Scots, hoped Elizabeth I might help her regain her throne.
- **B** Mary, Queen of Scots, had no faith that Elizabeth I might help her.

16 **How are people chosen for a jury?**

   A Randomly, from the electoral register

   B Randomly, from the lottery

   C People apply to be on a jury

   D They are appointed by legal professionals

17 **Cowes on the Isle of Wight is most famous in a sporting context for which of the following?**

   A Rowing

   B Sailing

   C Fishing championships

   D Surfing

18 **How old must you be to drive a car or motorcycle?**

   A 16

   B 17

   C 25

   D 70

19 **Why did a large number of Russian and Polish Jews come to Britain between 1870 and 1914?**

   A To look for work

   B To escape persecution

   C To buy cotton from British merchants

   D To learn English

20 **Which of these is not a famous poet?**

   A William Wordsworth

   B Alfred Lord Tennyson

   C Percy Shelley

   D Lucian Freud

21 **Which of James II's relatives were strictly Protestant?**

- **A** Brothers
- **B** Sisters
- **C** Daughters
- **D** Aunts and uncles

22 **Which TWO of the following are responsibilities for members of Parliament (MPs)?**

- **A** To represent everyone in their constituency
- **B** To support all government decisions and laws
- **C** To scrutinise and comment on the government's activities
- **D** To only represent constituents who voted for them

23 **Pressure and lobby groups represent the interests of which TWO of the following?**

- **A** Minor political parties
- **B** Foreign ambassadors
- **C** Business organisations
- **D** Campaigning organisations

24 **At what time is the two-minute silence observed on Remembrance Sunday?**

- **A** 11am
- **B** Noon
- **C** 3pm
- **D** 5pm

ANSWERS: PRACTICE TEST 19

			Handbook reference	Study Guide reference
1	A	A Danish king of England	33	39
2	B	The Speaker	131–2	137–8
3	A	The lords, the commons and the clergy	36–7	42–3
4	A	True	35	41
5	B	False	143	149
6	D	Lawrence of Arabia	109	115
7	B	Buying recycled products whenever possible	164	170
	C	Recycling waste when possible		
8	A	Divorce	83–4	89–90
9	C	129	133–7	139–43
10	A	Tribespeople from Northern Europe	31–3	37–40
11	D	Australia	53–5	59–61
12	C	First World War	104–6	110–2
13	C	Hannukah	89	95
14	D	Cricket	94	100
15	A	Mary, Queen of Scots hoped Elizabeth I might help her regain her throne.	43	49
16	A	Randomly, from the electoral register	148	154
17	B	Sailing	96	102
18	B	17	157	163
19	B	To escape persecution	59	65
20	D	Lucian Freud	104–6	110–2
21	C	Daughters	49	55
22	A	To represent everyone in their constituency	128	134
	C	To scrutinise and comment on the government's activities		
23	C	Business organisations	132	138
	D	Campaigning organisations		
24	A	11am	90	96

PRACTICE TEST 20

1 Is the statement below TRUE or FALSE?
The Scottish Exhibition and Conference Centre is in Edinburgh.

A True

B False

2 Which TWO of the following are famous plays by William Shakespeare?

A The Duchess of Malfi

B Romeo and Juliet

C A Midsummer Night's Dream

D Dr Faustus

3 In which British city is the Royal Crescent?

A Bath

B Exeter

C Edinburgh

D Cardiff

4 During which period of the Christian calendar is it traditional to fast?

A Easter

B Christmas

C Lent

D Advent

5 By the middle of the 15th century, what had happened to the last of the Welsh rebellions?

A They had been defeated by the English

B They had been contained within Wales

C They were victorious over the English armies

D They were abandoned because they were too expensive

6   Which British Admiral was killed at the Battle of Trafalgar?

A Napoleon

B Nelson

C Sir Francis Drake

D Duke of Wellington

7   Which of the following statements is correct?

A Civil law relates to crimes that are investigated by the police.

B Civil law relates to disputes between people.

8   Who was responsible for building the Tower of London?

A William the Conqueror

B Edward I

C Henry VIII

D Elizabeth I

9   Who is the only Briton to have won the Tour de France cycle race?

A Sir Chris Hoy

B Sir Bradley Wiggins

C Mark Cavendish

D Reg Harris

10   Is it legal to send a girl abroad for circumcision or cutting?

A Yes, if it is legal in the country to which she is sent

B No, it is illegal in the UK to send a girl abroad for circumcision or cutting

11   Does the Council of Europe have the power to make laws?

A Yes, but it does not use these powers often

B No, but it can draft agreements known as conventions and charters

12 **William Beveridge briefly served as an MP and was subsequently leader in the House of Lords for which political party?**

- **A** The Labour Party
- **B** The Liberal Party
- **C** The Conservative Party
- **D** The Green Party

13 **Halloween is regarded historically as which of the following?**

- **A** A Christian festival
- **B** A Muslim festival
- **C** A Pagan festival
- **D** A Sikh festival

14 **Where in Ireland did the English government encourage Scottish and English Protestants to settle during the reigns of Elizabeth I and James I?**

- **A** Ulster
- **B** Dublin
- **C** Cork
- **D** Armagh

15 **A famous boat race for rowers is contested on the River Thames each year between which TWO university teams?**

- **A** Cambridge and London
- **B** Edinburgh and Oxford
- **C** Edinburgh and London
- **D** Cambridge and Oxford

16 Penicillin was developed into a usable drug by Howard Florey and which other scientist?

- **A** Stephen Hawking
- **B** Marie Curie
- **C** Albert Einstein
- **D** Ernst Chain

17 Which artist, born in 1937, is famous for his contribution to the 'pop art' movement of the 1960s?

- **A** Lucian Freud
- **B** John Petts
- **C** David Hockney
- **D** Robert Lenkiewicz

18 Members of the Northern Ireland Assembly have worked together successfully since which year?

- **A** 2000
- **B** 2003
- **C** 2007
- **D** 2011

19 Which of these is not a UK regional language?

- **A** Welsh
- **B** Irish Gaelic
- **C** Gaelic
- **D** Kentish

20 Which of the statements below is not correct?

○ **A** More women than men study at university.

○ **B** There are now more female MPs than male MPs.

○ **C** Employment opportunities for women are much greater than they were in the past.

○ **D** Women work in all sectors of the economy.

21 Is the statement below TRUE or FALSE?
Ellie Simmonds is a Paralympian and was the youngest member of the British team at the 2008 games.

○ **A** True

○ **B** False

22 Is the statement below TRUE or FALSE?
Hospitals often need donated blood to help people who are ill or injured.

○ **A** True

○ **B** False

23 In the Church of Scotland, who is the Moderator?

○ **A** A key figure who is responsible for all relations with the Church of England

○ **B** A financial overseer who has overall responsibility for the accounts of the Church

○ **C** The spiritual leader of the Church, who is appointed for life

○ **D** The chairperson of the General Assembly, who is appointed for one year only and often speaks on behalf of the Church

24 Emmeline Pankhurst, who was born in Manchester in 1858, had a role in establishing which TWO organisations for women's rights?

○ **A** The Women's Voting Council

○ **B** The Women's Franchise League

○ **C** The Female Democratic Organisation

○ **D** The Women's Social and Political Union

ANSWERS: PRACTICE TEST 20

			Handbook reference	Study Guide reference
1	B	False	97–9	103–5
2	B	Romeo and Juliet	44	50
	C	A Midsummer Night's Dream		
3	A	Bath	102–3	108–9
4	C	Lent	88	94
5	A	They had been defeated by the English	35	41
6	B	Nelson	56–7	62–3
7	B	Civil law relates to disputes between people.	144–5	150–1
8	A	William the Conqueror	120	126
9	B	Sir Bradley Wiggins	92–3	98–9
10	B	No, it is illegal in the UK to send a girl abroad for circumcision or cutting	155	161
11	B	No, but it can draft agreements known as conventions and charters	143	149
12	B	The Liberal Party	71	77
13	C	A Pagan festival	90	96
14	A	Ulster	45	51
15	D	Cambridge and Oxford	96	102
16	D	Ernst Chain	70–1	76–7
17	C	David Hockney	101	107
18	C	2007	133–7	139–43
19	D	Kentish	82	88
20	B	There are now more female MPs than male MPs.	83–4	89–90
21	A	True	92–3	98–9
22	A	True	162	168
23	D	The chairperson of the General Assembly, who is appointed for one year only and often speaks on behalf of the Church	85	91
24	B	The Women's Franchise League	62	68
	D	The Women's Social and Political Union		

WELL DONE!

You've just taken 20 full tests.

Best of luck for your official Life in the UK test.

Let us know how it goes at
www.lifeintheuk.net/feedback

We'd love to hear your experiences, good or bad, or any suggestions you have to help us make our products better.

GET THE BRITTEST APP

Take practice tests wherever you go with
hundreds of questions and randomised
practice tests in your hand.

The essential revision aid for anyone on the move.
Find out more at **www.lifeintheuk.net/app**